HOW GOES IT WITH
AMERICA

IN THE INTERESTS OF EDUCATIONAL AND SOCIETAL REFORM

HARRY GAEL MICHAELS

How Goes it With America
Copyright © 2023 by Harry Gael Michaels

ISBN
978-1-961250-46-8 (Paperback)
978-1-961250-48-2 (eBook)
978-1-961250-47-5 (Hardcover)

How Goes It With America

In the Interests of Educational and Societal Reform

Other books by Harry Gael Michaels

An Educational and Family Friendly Prospectus

*The State of the Republic: How the Misadventures
of U.S. Policy since WWII Have Led
to the Quagmire of Today's Economic,
Social and Political Disappointments*

*Wings Over Normandy: A WWII Story
of the B-26 and One Man that Flew It*

*Reflections on Institutional Catholic-ism:
A Critical Perspective*

The Quest for Peace: Quelling the Rash of Violence

Coping With Life: A Study in Adaptation

TABLE OF CONTENTS

HOW GOES IT WITH AMERICA

In the Interests of Educational Reform

(A 2011 Revision)

Endorsed by:

Arnold A. Lazarus, Ph.D., ABPP

Executive Director, The Lazarus Institute,

Skillman, New Jersey

GOALS FOR EDUCATING CHILDREN

Standards of the Fulton County School System, State of Georgia

TO:

1. Value life-long learning.
2. Value a world perspective of order and cooperation.
3. Value the essential dignity of all people.
4. Value one's family, community, and nationhood.
5. Develop self-confidence to reach personal potential.
6. Assume responsibility for personal development.
7. Think critically and problem solve.
8. Set personal, academic, and career goals.
9. Pursue health and well-being.
10. Understand and accept family roles and obligations.
11. Respect diversity and freedom.
12. Exhibit tolerance for differences.
13. Demonstrate multi-cultural awareness.
14. Work collaboratively.
15. Integrate and use technology effectively.
16. Demonstrate transferable employment skills.

17. Access and manage resources.
18. Apply acquired knowledge to everyday life.
19. Exhibit organizational skills.
20. Listen actively.
21. Speak articulately.
22. Express ideas in writing and competently.
23. Read critically.

It is believed that this book is appropriate for review by the following professional journals: The National Association of School Psychologists, American School Board Journals, Contemporary Issues in Early Childhood, National Center for Transforming School Counseling and School Library journal.

Dedications:

Many will testify that there are well functioning schools and school systems in the United States; however, this book addresses the many that are not. My intention is to provide some thoughts and teaching points as well as a guidance manual in dedication to all those who believe we have a vested interest in providing quality education, guidance, and a successful political society for the progeny of America. This book, therefore, is dedicated to the educators, leaders, and parents of school age children of America.

This book is also dedicated to my wife Bea whose keen and perceptive mind and loving heart has helped me with the vagaries of my own—and to my children, Lisa, Chris, and Julie, who thrive valiantly and face life's adversities and challenges with courage and faith and love.

This important and engaging book covers educational incompetency in the U.S. at the primary/elementary and secondary levels, as well as teaching points and guidance for students in the late teens and early 20s. It includes chapter summaries and review questions.

Teaching points are relevant to the fields of Civics, U.S. History, and Sociology. Guidance features are relevant to Counseling and Life Adjustment. It is my hope that this book will be widely disseminated because of its relevance to current problems of improving educational excellence and effectively orienting young people to the complexities and challenges of modern living.

Arnold A. Lazarus, Ph.D., ABPP
Distinguished Professor Emeritus of Psychology Rutgers University Executive Director, The Lazarus Institute, Skillman,
New Jersey.

CHAPTER 1

While pondering the state of my homeland, I could not help comparing and contrasting the America I grew up during the '30s and '40s with America since WWII. I have often been puzzled with questions such as why are we in the condition we are in today and how did we get that way? Where are we going? Why are the people so frustrated with their government? Why do children live in such fear—even to go to school—and why is there such worry about the future of America's progeny? Why is there so much violence? In short, HOW GOES IT WITH AMERICA, and is there hope for the future? The following is a journal of the problems, highlights, and events of the past 50 years that, at least, helps me to some degree explain what has happened in this country to bring us to where we are today—and what we might do about it.

On April 20, 1999, a shooting occurred at Columbine High School in Littleton, Colorado—a shooting that was perpetrated by two teenage boys of the same student body. The American people had once again been shocked into a state of grief and helpless confusion. How could this happen in America? Why is this only one of many such incidents that has been occurring in recent years? With every event of school violence we go through spasms of gut wrenching grief and anguish and the first voices we hear are the self-styled experts who get on the air and tell us we must get rid of all guns, or no, we must put safety locks on guns, or no, we must keep guns out of the hands of criminals, or no, we must prosecute parents whose children get their hands on guns and kill with them. Others say we must tighten down security at the schools and have more armed police walking the halls along with metal detectors at the doors. Some would say that we must arm students and teachers so they can defend themselves in the event of a terrorist attack.

School violence has become a kind of barometric pressure indicator of the degree of social unrest and disorder in the population in general and could be thought of as a top priority concern. School violence and, indeed, violence in the society at large, has become a manifestation of the serious underlying fear and despair that has pervaded our society more threateningly than the externalized worries of Americans during WWII. Professional thinking agrees that kids who are the most unstable and vulnerable (and that population does not have to be very large) are the ones that will break with reality and act out in dramatic form the terrifying sense of alienation and lack of national social morality that has gripped this nation during the past 50 years. We have become an uptight, over-stressed, angry, and violent society where goodwill and trust based on a handshake has gone the way of the winds. Our culture has become so diffused that we hardly recognize who we are anymore. Our essential strength is freedom but freedom with social responsibility.

It does appear that we are sacrificing our national integrity and freedoms by over-accommodation and appeasement of every excess and digression of human dignity that can be thought up by the aberrant in our society—all, presumably, in the interests of civil rights and the first amendment. It does seem that we have generated a culture of those who feel they are entitled to liberties and freedoms without inculcating a sense of accountability. Parents often fail to take responsibility for the spiritual and moral training of their children. Political leadership has subverted the basic ethics upon which our way of life was founded and then attempts to deceive the people as though they are mindless fools.

Children in school have had to live with a fear of disease and violence that was unknown prior to the 1960s. Violence and sexually transmitted diseases threaten their lives while television and films portray an alluring and titillating attraction to thoughtless sex and violence. Hospital emergency rooms have been overwhelmed by the number of gunshot and stab wounds among young people in the central cities of his country. Teenage suicide and homicide rates have risen alarmingly. In the 1950s, student's transgressions in school were typically running in the halls, chewing gum in class, throwing spitballs and an occasional fist-fight; whereas, by the 1980s, children began threatening other students and even teachers with guns and knives and, in some cases, fulfilling their threats. The incidence of despondency among youth has increased and lack of trust toward people representing authority has steadily risen since the 1960s and the "dawn of Aquarius."

At the same time, school administrators have become so intimidated by the fear of litigation that they cringe from taking steps to actively intervene with those students who are clearly heading for trouble. I recently talked to an elementary teacher in an upscale neighborhood school district who noticed a little boy displaying disturbing sexual simulations in her classroom. When she reported the incident to the administrator, he advised her to "cool it" because the father was a prominent attorney. When we have a Jonesboro or a Littleton we wonder why an adolescent in a desperate and disconnected final spasm of despair and destruction will scream out in repressed rage, "LOOK AT ME."

There was a time in the 1960s before laws relating to juveniles were changed to protect their rights, when the juvenile probation officer served a very useful role in the community by intervening on behalf of young people and parents and helping school personnel deal with more difficult kids. Much good work was done in counseling as an adjunct to law enforcement. Kids were able to learn that authority figures could be fair and friendly as well as firm in their resolve to uphold the law. Recidivism rates were very low then and a violent crime against a person was rarity. But the most difficult and prophetic cases were those described as "beyond control," which is to say they were beyond the control of parental influence and supervision. In fact, those parents, in order to pursue their own interests, relinquished their authority and supervision responsibilities and allowed their children more power over their own lives than they had the maturity to handle. Those were the cases in which parents would come in saying that their child was simply out of control, would not take supervision from them, ignored any attempts at correction or punishment and showed no respect whatsoever. They wanted the probation officer, as a symbol of authority, to take charge and redirect the misguided behavior of years of neglectful parenting. This is not to say that these parents were bad or incompetent people. They were, however, caught up in the cultural stresses and influences of modern American life; i.e., both parents working to maintain a desirable standard of living.

The increasing incidence of single parent homes without the assistance of nearby extended family members and inadequate support services in the community became the norm. The unfortunate result was that those parents were unknowingly and, in many cases, simply unaware that they were virtually ignoring the emotional and spiritual needs of their children. Such children were often left to their own devices for entertaining themselves along with unearned money and privileges. Typically this type of kid would vent his anger and fear and feelings of abandonment by attempting to destroy property. It hadn't yet reached the level of destroying people but with our liberal permissiveness and denial it could have been predicted.

In our educational history teachers were respected and admired members of the community. They were looked upon as professionals and the respect was relayed through the parents by their children and when a child was reprimanded in the school, the parent backed up the teacher unless there was some blatant misbehavior on the part of the school official— and that was very rare. It is entirely different now. Children have rights and parents have a scapegoat if things don't go well. In earlier times, a disorderly student was given a second chance to amend his behavior or, if not, out he went to some other form of training such as a school/work/ranch program, a detention facility that was designed to instill self-discipline and respect for authority or, if the youth was old enough, an enlistment in the military service—or even an early release from school on the condition that he would have a job. The classroom was a place for teaching and learning— not an institution for correctional or mental health issues. Before 1960, common disciplinary problems were easily handled by a talk with the teacher, principal, or a parent, in that order. In more complicated cases, a probation officer could be called in to assist and offer some supervision. Those measures were usually quite effective. Today, misbehavior can range from drug abuse, to rape, to assault and extortion, to murder and mayhem and the measures for insuring safety and security must be much more extreme.

Misbehavior problems had to be tolerated in the schools and even in the classroom; thereby, diminishing the degree of time and attention the teacher could devote to teaching. Classroom control became a priority over instruction and gave rise to the phrase, "academic baby-sitting." At the same time, parents took less and less interest in helping to coordinate activities with their children in school, perhaps because of both having to work to maintain a standard of living and also because of the rising incidence of single parent homes giving rise to the other new term, "latch-key kid."

Furthermore, because of the advent of more emphasis on the rights of children, parents became reluctant to take a more active stance when it came to their child's emotional, social and moral development. Parents gave up their power and authority as parents and transferred guidance and training over to the school and the church, which, in either case, were ill-equipped to assume. Kids could come to school wearing a swastika and alien clothing, but never a religious symbol. Even a silent prayer was thrown out as too prejudicial. Teachers were afraid to lay a hand on a child even as an innocent gesture of affection. An expression like that could be misinterpreted by a hostile parent and the school could be in for a large lawsuit. A pall of mistrust and fear had settled over the country like bad air.

There is no doubt that much good came out of the civil rights movement, but exaggerated reactions and bad judgments on the part of some of our judges and politicians led to violent counter-reactions on both sides of the spectrum. As an example, forced busing as an attempt to force integration of the

African-American population was one of the first bad judgments. It meant pulling children out of their neighborhood schools in order to bus them across town to strange schools in strange parts of the city. This usually took hours of wasted time. Kids from less adequate schools and neighborhoods would then be transported across town to better facilities only to be returned again at the end of the day to their depressed environments. It would have made more sense, it seems to me, to first improve the schools and neighborhoods of those whose educational and environmental conditions were lacking in acceptable standards and then allow the process of integration to occur in a more compatible way. Another act of bad judgment that we are now becoming more aware of, and which is changing through more enlightened legislation, was an over-indulgent and crippling welfare system. This was to further demoralize large portions of the population and instill attitudes of dependency and hostility. Being administered to "on the dole" may appeal to those inclined towards laziness or psychological inadequacy, but it does nothing to enhance their self-esteem or sense of productivity.

Families have become more fragmented and children are not given the attention and supervision they require in order to grow strong and purposeful. There are more young people trying to survive on the streets of our large cities than ever before. Young girls become mothers trying to use their infants to fill the awful void of loneliness and emptiness in their lives or resort to prostitution as the only survival skill in their uncaring world. It does appear that in the past 50 years we have departed from a sense of national integrity and too many young people, consequently, have become dismayed and confused as to just what this nation's ideals truly are.

In defense of the schools, it must be said that during the 1960s some dramatic changes began to occur in relating to juveniles. Laws were changed to accommodate what were seen as the rights of children. This was a noble attempt to correct many of the child abuses of the past-and there were many as we all know. The schools were charged with responsibilities never before seen and became accountable not only for education but also for dealing with serious disruptive behavior, emotional illness, family disturbance, and disabilities of every kind. School systems were required to develop more and more categories of special education programs with the complicating factors of mainstreaming along with legally mandated procedures for diagnostic selection. The laws mandated that the school provide instruction to all students in a mainstream mode as much as possible so as not to discriminate among them. Administrators often became embroiled in litigation with parents who were girded with legal support when it came to an unhappy placement of a child with special needs. Many parents would intensely resist accepting their child's limitations. In addition, there was a continual influx of immigrants from foreign countries with differing languages and cultures that had to be accommodated as well.

In too many instances the school systems of America have broken down and there is a serious lack of quality. As a matter of fact there are too many schools and school systems in which up to forty percent of the students drop out before graduating high school because they are bored, confused, afraid, or hopelessly frustrated. We see in the news the squalid and dangerous environments in which too many children must endure and survive because of what Jon Kozol and others have described as the "dead zones" of filth and poverty. How can we expect children to learn and grow strong in such an environment if we no longer expect adults to work in such conditions? Many who doggedly "hang in there" do so with the futile hope that the high school diploma will somehow afford them the possibility of a successful job and an enriching life only to discover later that the coveted piece of paper, which testifies to their acquired competence, is not a true representation of acquired skills and knowledge. In a 1991 publication authored by Edward Fiske, entitled "Smart Schools, Smart Kids," it was reported that the New York telephone company in 1987 had to screen 57,000 applicants in order to find 2,000 with entry-level skills for operators and repair technicians. With such realities, we see every day on the six o'clock news the horrendous violence and disorder that comes from the anger, frustration, and despair of those other thousands who were rejected. They find solace and commiseration for their crushed esteem with the escapism of drugs and the resentful acting-out of criminal behavior. This nation cannot tolerate such a waste of youthful resources. In this society what is not an asset becomes a liability and this world today is too competitive to absorb such liability. In today's marketplace, countries will likely fail or prosper on the capacity of its citizens to think and innovate and use technical skills as well as to function well as a society. Education, therefore, ought to be a preparation for a life of competence, interest, and contribution.

In America there is a great diversity of human resources with differing gifts, talents, and levels of ability and since our political system requires an educated and knowledgeable populace, it lays on the public school systems a heavy professional responsibility to help students learn and achieve as individuals rather than as a mass of pupils in a lock-step, factory like model that was effective in serving the educational needs during the time of our industrial revolution. Authors such as William G. Webster, in his book, "Learner-Centered Principalship," and Retired Major General John Stanford in his book, "Victory In Our Schools," referenced in the Bibliography, both have had superintendent responsibilities and are telling us for the importance of school principals taking a more active role as master teacher with their teachers and that it is imperative that teachers be elevated to the professional status that was originally intended. These considerations will be further addressed in Chapter 3.

CHAPTER SUMMARY

- Chapter 1 attempts to indicate a trend toward serious misbehavior in the schools highlighted by the shootings at Columbine High School in 1999, seemingly as a result of the fear and despair among the least stable in the younger elements of the population.
- There is evidence that political leadership has deteriorated to the point that there exists a feeling of loss of national integrity and trust among the people of America.
- Comparing misbehavior of the 1950s with that of the 1990s shows a significant increase of the violence and disarray not only in the schools, but in society in general.
- Many parents have lost confidence in their authority to lead and guide their children and much of this responsibility has been left to the public institutions.
- The schools have become burdened with accountabilities far beyond their original mandate to educate in that the schools are now responsible for dealing with large classroom populations, foreign cultures and languages, mental/behavioral and family issues, more diversified special education needs, and diminishing funding.
- Attempts to redress these problems with legislation and court imposed mandates has only exacerbated the difficulties and school administrators have become embroiled in

litigation over issues of parental discontent and children are being thrust into adulthood poorly trained and prepared for useful citizenship.

REVIEW QUESTIONS

- What important event occurred in 1999 that prompted this author to write this book? Describe what happened.
- Do you think misbehavior in the schools has been increasing or decreasing?
- Do you think the schools are meeting the challenges of preparing young people for successful adult lives?
- Do children in school feel confident in American society and government today? If not, why?

CHAPTER 2

When World War II came to an end in 1945, historians were suggesting that the coming era would be called the Age of Anxiety because for the first time the human race had to face the possibility of nuclear annihilation. We did not anticipate the anxiety that would pervade this country due to the social deterioration of the post WWII era. However, we emerged from WWII as an unequaled world power and confident of controlling the nuclear genie. The United States had decisively won perhaps the most significant war in history and then began to reach out to its conquered enemies to help them in their recovery and reconstruction.

At the close of WWII in Europe and the discovery of the suicidal remains of Adolph Hitler and his new bride, Eva Braun, in a bunker under his Reich Chancellery, Germany was in a state of total destruction and collapse. Then in 1948, under the Marshall Plan conceived by General George C. Marshall. President Truman's Secretary of State, C-54 cargo planes from the U.S. were dispatched on a round-the-clock schedule flying into Berlin with vital supplies for the devastated German people and helping them restore their shattered homeland to some semblance of order and recovery while at Nuremberg, Nazi war criminals were being prosecuted for unspeakable crimes against humanity. It was during this time that the full horror of the death camps came to light. As a result of the Yalta (Feb. 1945) and the Potsdam (Aug. 1945) conferences, a decision was made by the allied governments, to acquiesce to the Premier of the Soviet Union, Joseph Stalin, and his demands for control of East Berlin and Eastern Germany at the end of the War. From there it was rather easy for Stalin to annex the rest of Eastern Europe as well as the tiny countries of Latvia, Estonia, and Lithuania. Other concessions were made as well to Stalin in the Far East. He was given control of the Kurile Islands and South Sakhalin Island north of Japan, the port city of Darien and Port Arthur, as well as control of the Manchurian railway. This was his reward for entering the war against Japan six days before the unconditional surrender of the Japanese on the deck of the battleship Missouri in Tokyo Bay. As an aside, it is interesting to note that in recent years there have been friendly meetings at some of the Pacific battle sites between veterans of the U.S. and the Japanese. A documentary was broadcast on American television over 60 years after bombing of Pearl Harbor in 1941 in which veteran Japanese pilot, who took part in the attack, was met by a veteran American pilot at Pearl Harbor on the memorial of the USS Arizona, in which they recalled their part in the event in friendship and goodwill.

After the Japanese surrender, General Douglas MacArthur set about establishing a new post-war democratic political system in that devastated country and the Emperor Hirohito was no longer regarded as the descendant of the Sun God. Japanese citizens could now look upon his face while they cleaned up the devastation of the war and the utter obliteration of Nagasaki and Hiroshima, the first two cities ever to be destroyed by nuclear weapons. Even though MacArthur was a political conservative, most of those working under him were liberal democrats who were following the deceased President Roosevelt's "New Deal." This was recognition of labor unions and the notion of using collective bargaining to settle labor-management differences, such as wages, work hours, or working conditions. Generally, the New Deal allowed for private enterprise under the guidance of the government.

Back home, returning veterans had begun enjoying their rewards of victory by starting families and continuing their education on the GI Bill. All over America college campuses were bordered by Quonset huts and barrack-type living quarters for married vets and their families. Young kids were now going to college with older veterans and could find themselves sitting next to a war-wise former officer or enlisted man from any branch of the Armed Forces. Adequate housing was quite accessible at a three percent, thirty year fixed mortgage or less on a VA loan. Things were booming as "Rosie the Riveter" relinquished her job for a returning serviceman and women went back into the home. New cars, toasters, and refrigerators hit the market and wartime ration stamp books went out in the trash. The price of a Coca-Cola was a nickel; you could buy a new car for

$900.00, and buy a new house for $9,000.00. The cost of a postage stamp was three cents.

The United Nations Organization was formed in San Francisco in 1945 and its first major challenge was the Korean conflict that began in 1950. Communist-inspired Koreans from the north, who had seen the Communist takeover of China in 1949, launched an all-out attack on the southern provinces of Korea. It was believed that the incursion of North Korea, under the Russian installed Kim II Sung, into South Korea under the leadership of the American installed Syngman Rhee, a devout Christian and with a Ph.D. in politics from Princeton, could trigger an Armageddon if nuclear weapons were to be used. A plan, therefore, of containment and resistance had to be implemented without provoking the hordes of Communist Chinese to enter the fray and also to avoid resorting to nuclear escalation. With this delicate balance in mind, President Truman flew out to Wake Island (1951) to meet with General MacArthur in order to relieve him as Supreme Commander in Korea. President Truman believed that MacArthur was committed to launching a total invasion of North Korea that would take him into Manchuria and thereby inciting a major conflict with China. The new era, however, dictated a policy of containment of aggressive adversaries rather than the achievement of total victory and unconditional surrender as was the case in WWII. It was later to be learned that the containment policy of Soviet aggression, as fathered by George F. Kennan, head of the State Department's first policy planning staff (1947-1950), was intended to be political and diplomatic rather than military. However, the subsequent reconfiguration of this policy under the "hawkish" advice of Paul Nitze (National Security Council under President Harry Truman), led to the military involvements in Korea and Vietnam to curb the "domino effect" of Communist insurgence.

As we entered the '50s, the Soviet Union, our ally in WWII, was now being seen as a deadly adversary following the deliverance of nuclear secret documents by Ethel and Julius Rosenberg (1951) and the subsequent buildup of nuclear weapons under Stalin's sinister leadership. Children were taught to "duck and cover" in response to an attack by the Soviets. The Strategic Air Command carried out 24-hour operations in which heavy bombers loaded with nuclear weapons were constantly airborne in rotating shifts. There was also a frenetic buildup of land-based intercontinental ballistic missile sites and stealthy nuclear-armed submarines prowled the oceans on both sides. Then in October of 1957, the Soviet Union launched Sputnik, the first satellite to orbit the earth, and as we heard the peculiar beep as it circled the globe, the country was shocked into an awareness of how deficient our schools had been in teaching math and science. Movies such as *"On the Beach"* and *"Fail-Safe"* dramatized the cataclysmic possibilities of a military miscalculation. The idea was that any attack would be met with devastating retaliation and so the policy was called "MAD" for Mutually Assured Destruction. Senator Joe McCarthy of Wisconsin was conducting "communists behind every bush" inquisitions in the U.S. Senate and many people in education, government, and entertainment had their reputations ruined by association and innuendo.

Following WWII, Americans were said to see themselves as innocent and invincible— innocent in that we were on the side of righteousness and goodness and invincible in that we were heroic and un-conquerable. This was demonstrated in the television shows of the 1950s. The country seemed to revel in the innocent and naïve family life of Ozzie and *Harriet, Father Knows Best, Leave It To Beaver*, and the most popular, *Happy Days*, as well as the invincible American hero "westerns", such as *Gun Smoke, The Virginian*, and *Rawhide*. At the same time, a new form of irrepressible music emerged—the rock beat. Chubby Checker, Elvis Presley, Jerry Lee Lewis, Little Richard, and Buddy Holley, to name a few, were giving music a new sense of emotional expression and displacing the dreamy, sentimental ballads of the WWII years. The Beatles were forming a style of music in Liverpool that was going to ride the crest of a social revolution that would eventually see its zenith at the great Woodstock "happening" in Bethel, New York. "Beatniks" of the '50s were giving way to "Hippies" of the '60s. Jack Kerouac and Allen Ginsberg offered young people a kind of ragbag philosophy of rebellion and alienation from the established American culture. Joan Baez took us back to a purer and more distilled time in American life in the form of rarefied folk music and, at the same time, she and Ira Sandperl, her political mentor, established the Institute for the Study of Non-Violence in Carmel Valley, California in deference to the earlier Mahatma Gandhi movement in India.

As we entered the 1960s, there appeared to be a "Crossing of the Rubicon" of social change in the United States. In the major cities, particularly in San Francisco, drug experimentation and "free love" offered the illusion of creating a new world by "tuning in, turning on, and dropping out" as espoused by the drop-out Harvard Psychology Professor, Dr. Timothy Leary. At the same time, a kind of psychological regression to earlier times in American history seemed to capture the imagination of the people. We lost ourselves in the folk music of Peter, Paul and Mary, the Weavers, Pete Seeger, Bob Dylan, and Arlo Guthrie—the son of Woody Guthrie.

When we traded in the sensible conservatism of Dr. Benjamin Spock for the "spacey" liberalism of Dr. Timothy Leary, we began a long slide into the diffusion of the American culture as we knew it. A redress of the inequalities of the past among selective minority groups took on attitudes of hyper-atonement for specific historical ethnic transgressions. African-American militancy, as espoused by Malcom X in the South and in the form of the Black Panthers in the West, emerged under the leadership of Eldridge Cleaver and Angela Davis. Mario Savio shouted and stormed at Sather Gate and the U.C. Berkeley campus became a focal point for crusades against educational and political establishments while an African-American woman in Montgomery, Alabama by the name of Rosa Parks refused to go to the back of the bus. What followed were increasingly intense confrontations between the African-American people and authority figures. A young visionary preacher by name of Martin Luther King, Jr. took a position at the head of a movement for equal rights and non-violent civil disobedience and prayed for people to be judged on the "content of their character rather than the color of their skin." In 1964, Civil Rights legislation seemed to promise a fruition of the "dreams" of MLK and the African-American people and, at the same time, would presage the foreboding of difficult times ahead. Unfortunately, instead of getting King's message, the African-American society began aligning itself in distinctly oppositional camps and referring to itself divisively as "Black" as opposed to "White." In March of 1991, a young African-American by the name of Rodney King was the subject of police brutality after a DUI stop and it happened to be caught on video by a bystander. The result was catastrophic. Resentments smoldered and then erupted in the devastating Watt riots of South Central Los Angeles almost tearing that city apart and Rodney King, himself, appealed for a cessation of violence in his pathetic statement, "Can't we just all get along." In all this confusion and divisive anger, Blacks (as they preferred to be called) were invested with inordinate and indulgent deference while ignoring the fact that most all immigrant groups that originally entered this country or even those indigenous to it were oppressed in some form. In the Black populations of America there developed a bifurcated attitude toward American society. On the one hand, there were those who looked upon their U.S. citizenship as an opportunity to strive and to become assimilated into the American culture. They were to make contributions as responsible members of the society as others had done. At the same time, there were those who chose to revel in their rage and feelings of victimization. The latter groups were to present a huge problem because their demonstrated attitude of belligerence and hostility was one of getting back and getting even for the sins of the past and the battle cry was "racism." Those who were to persist in this oppositional attitude seemed not to realize that their best interests lie in non-violent persuasion, as their great leader MLK had taught, rather than in attitudes of paranoid hostility. The enslavement and exploitation of the African Negro was a terrible thing; however, Negro slavery was not the only form of indentured servitude in this country. Consider the plight of the Chinese, many of whom were abducted and brought to this country to be used to build the railroads in the West, and the Irish immigrants who built the railroads in the East suffered much the same indignities as the Negro—and don't forget the indigenous Native American Indians who were so badly treated and demoralized that most now exist only in a state of helpless and depressed dependency. The Negro people were not the only in a state of helpless and depressed dependency. The Negro people were not the only ethnic group to suffer oppression and exploitation in America. It is true that no other ethnic group was brought to this country in chains and sold in a public square, but we must also remember that the greatest suffering this country had ever known occurred during our own Civil War (1861-1865) in its struggle to emancipate the African-Americans from the bonds of slavery and tyranny. The subsequent struggle of prejudicial intolerance and racism that was to follow was a moral issue and a legal one and should have been dealt with as such. Once it became the law of the land that the African-American was entitled to the same civil/legal considerations as the rest of the population, issues of prejudicial intolerance ought not to have become a source of civil manipulation. It could be argued that legislating personal morality, social sensitivity, and good manners is a pointless endeavor.

In spite of all the unfairness with which some ethnic groups were treated in this country, some of their own served brilliantly and courageously to defend the United Stated in time of war. Reference the Navaho Code Talkers of WWII who made important contributions to winning the war in the Pacific against the Japanese and the segregated Tuskegee Airmen (a group of African-American fighter pilots) who escorted bombers over Europe in a protective umbrella that was completely successful in fighting off enemy air attacks. Japanese-Americans who were imprisoned in isolation camps during WWII gave their sons to the Armed Forces who served magnificently in the struggle against the Nazi armies of Adolf Hitler and the African-American soldiers throughout American history stood tall with other ethnic groups in defense of freedom and the emancipation from slavery and the right to live as free men.

In my view, indulgent acquiescence, however, toward the African-American and then Hispanic groups selectively beginning in the 1960s threatened the integrity of what this nation had always represented, i.e., a society of hard working and industrious individuals, by tradition, but also a society of well-defined cultural mores and idealistic values that we shared with each other as a New World culture in trust and community interests. This is not to say that African-American and Hispanic groups were inherently incompetent to hold their own in America, but they did have a need for effective assistance and encouragement in the form of education and training and the opportunity to succeed. They did not need to be warehoused and custodialized in "projects" or administered to as helpless wards as in the case of the American Indians. Our liberalized "Great Society" programs only indulged and disavowed those particular groups as a way of dismissing the problem and perhaps atoning for a national sense of guilt.

The Great Society intentions were highly ambitious in a "social engineering" sense. It was intended to address the injustices perpetrated against minority groups with reference to civil rights and it did, which was good, but it also led to injustices toward those who were not allowed to compete for jobs because of "affirmative action" policies. Discrimination went the other way. A white person, highly qualified, could not get a job as a counselor in a community college because those jobs were given first to minority person who might have been less qualified. This was because of the civil rights legislation that attempted to redress the discrimination of the past. The "war on poverty" provided aid to families with dependent children in the form of housing projects and money and food stamps, but let to what some believe was further destruction of the African-American family. It encouraged women to have more children to get more money and it encouraged men to shirk on their responsibilities to father and provide for their children. In the education area, many federal resources were channeled into helping the learning handicapped and preparing young ones in the form of "head start" programs, but it seems that money was directed in such a way as not to be accountable for the year on anything in order to not have his quota reduced for the following year. It also seemed to play into legislation to relieve home owners of paying a fair share of taxes to support the schools. Health legislation benefited many, but most were older people on Medicare and those below the poverty line with Medicaid. On the other hand, the middle class working people began to suffer because of increasing costs of medical insurance. Consumer protection attempted to shore up deficiencies in business and industry but gave people a feeling of having a "big brother" always looking down on you. Government seemed to be everywhere and involved in our daily life. And finally, there was the issue of the environment. The movement to preserve the environment was a good thing. We were hearing of polluted lakes and streams and waste dumps of hazardous material that threatened the lives of children, but there, again, it seemed as though there was an over zealousness that made it hard for loggers to cut down trees and regulate the forests.

In San Francisco, Enrico Banducci's "Hungry Eye," located at 546 Broadway Street, was instrumental in starting the careers of Mort Sahl and Lenny Bruce, Ronnie Schell, Bill Cosby, the Kingston Trio, Vince Guaraldi, Glen Yarborough, Professor Irwin Corey, and the Mamas and the Pappas. It was "in" to take pot shots at the establishment and the "flower children" started gravitating to the corner of Height and Ashbury. What began there as an innocent experimentation with LSD, marijuana, and communal living under the pseudo-spiritual leadership of the drug gurus later became festooned with sickly flowers of hostility, disease, and "bad trips." It was a time of blasphemous defiance and misguided dissent. President John Kennedy was reluctantly sending "technical advisors" (1961) to assist the "Westernized" Vietnamese in the south with their struggle against the military insurgence of the Communist Vietnamese in the north. Senator J. William Fulbright of Arkansas and Senator Wayne Morse of Oregon presided over the Senate Foreign Relations Committee and daily made appeals to common sense and the Constitutional errors of committing U.S. Armed Forces to that Southeast Asia Civil War. They further tried to point out that our military involvement in Vietnam would be very weakly supported by SEATO, Southeast Asia Treaty Organization, and even questioned the constitutionality of our involvement in that alliance. All this fell on deaf ears because of the din of hysteria and confusion about stemming the "domino effect" of Communist aggression. The whole Southeast Asia situation put Kennedy in a difficult bind because of his reluctance to fully engage US troops in that emerging war. He had been burned by the "Bay of Pigs" fiasco in the early part of his administration and did not want to entertain any such future failures. In the 1960s, the Nation was in a state of extreme worry when it was learned in 1962 that the Soviets had installed long-range missiles in Cuba that could reach vital areas in the US. The new president, John F. Kennedy, ordered Soviet Premier Nikita Khrushchev to take them out unless there be certain retaliation that would likely lead to nuclear war. The whole world stood on the brink of global devastation. Fortunately, the matter was resolved when the U.S. agreed to withdraw its missile sites in Turkey and allowed Khrushchev to save face. A year later, in 1963, we were shocked and horrified by the assassination of President John F. Kennedy, and in 1968, a promising presidential aspirant, Robert "Bobby" Kennedy, and a charismatic leader of the civil rights movement, Martin Luther King Jr. were also assassinated.

In recent history, the American culture has undergone the diffusion of what once were valued traditions. At the same time, attempts to redress the wrongs of past injustices took on cataclysmic sweeps of change. An excessive liberalization of laws and "Great Society" welfare programs provided a special deference to those who would abuse the system or adapt to a further diminution of personal effectiveness and, at the same time,smolder with hostile/dependent resentment. Judicial systems and "due process of law" were indulgently administered to and even those who had been convicted of terrible crimes against humanity were regarded still as invested with the same rights and privileges as the law-abiding citizen. Endless appeals and shortened sentences for "good behavior" gave the sociopathically disposed tremendous manipulative advantages. In my view, excesses of the American Civil Liberties Union provided criminals in court with rights far beyond equal fairness with an offended plaintiff and prison confinement became couched with television, telephones, workout facilities, conjugal visits, weekend passes, and higher education in the law. In some cases, even those who were incarcerated received Social Security payments under Supplemental Security Income (SSI). Criminal justice began taking precedence over citizen justice.

Radical and poorly constructed legislation was impulsively implemented to make things right and equal for those who are thought to be the most oppressed. Instead of upgrading the quality of schools in the impoverished areas with a plan of gradual and consistent improvement, Judge W. Arthur Garrity Junior of the United States District Court for the District of Massachusetts, mandated children from "good" neighborhood schools to spend wasted hours on buses being transported to "bad" schools across town. Instead of a well-thought-out plan of education and training for impoverished minority groups, we launched an indulgent welfare program that only served to further incapacitate and demoralize people. This only served to breed dependency and resentment into many underprivileged Americans who could have been better served in more productive ways. Instead, we spotted African-American, Hispanic, and American Indians with "affirmative action" advantages further lowering standards of achievement and productivity while at the same time surreptitiously labeling them as inferior and incompetent. Tokenism and mediocrity were the standards of those years. Some benefited, true, we understand now that most did not. Anger, resentment, and dependency set the stage for a massive avoidance reaction with devastating flights from reality into a drug culture which had, in turn, unleashed the greatest social disorder this Nation has ever known as a new kind of violent crime was emerging on the American scene. Horrendous, irrational, and incomprehensible assaults even toward children began occurring with regularity. Military assault firearms with rapid-fire capability that were designed for war were being bought up and used regularly by dangerous individuals with criminal records because there was no effective control over these weapons. The National Rifle Association wielded tremendous power with their lobby in Congress and legislators backed off from taking responsible action. During this time there was an excessive liberalizing bias toward justice for criminal behavior and the California Supreme Court virtually allowed repeat violent offenders to walk the streets and continue to practice their monstrous profession—and the rest of the nation followed that insidious lead. We had not learned as a society that some twisted individuals commit their horrible crimes "so they can relieve tension, feel pleasure, and get a good night's sleep," as one inmate put it. This kind of indulgent "liberal" thinking was to also devalue the quality of education for young people because it became the right of errant and incorrigible children to remain mainstreamed in the classroom. Teachers had to spend much of their valuable teaching time controlling those who would not cooperate. The threat of litigation hung in the air like a bad smell and accountability in the form of increased bureaucratic paperwork further interfered with teacher effectiveness. In my experience, I discovered that school administrators found justification for increasing the ranks and their salaries. The teacher, who was the real professional, was caught in the backwater sludge and frustration that comes from a diminished status and impossible expectations. As classroom populations increase beyond the point for effective teaching, school funding for those who were the last fired might have to sweat out whether or not their contract would be renewed for the following year—even before they ever had a chance to make their contributions. The older and less effective teachers were protected by tenure.

During this time it became clear that disengagement from the Vietnam War was imperative. Our involvement had virtually torn this country apart and had come close to creating civil anarchy. In 1968, the Democratic Convention in Chicago had produced scenes reminiscent of Nazi Germany prior to the advent of WWII. After the election of Richard Nixon in 1969, President Nixon and Dr. Henry Kissinger, Secretary of State, had secretly orchestrated the bombing of Cambodia, creating further unrest and dissent among the American people. That same year, Neil Armstrong, the first man on the moon, saluted the world with, "One small step for a man, one giant step for mankind." The antiwar movement under the leadership of Jerry Rubin, the organizer of the VDC (Vietnam Day Committee), and Abby Hoffman, (and the Chicago 7) played important roles in the disruption of the 1968 Democratic National Convention in Chicago. Then in 1971, Daniel Ellsberg, Pentagon military analyst during the 60s, released the Pentagon Papers to the New York Times, which the Nixon administration attempted to bar from publication by court order. Then, on June 29, 1971, U.S. Senator Mike Gravel of Alaska entered 4,100 pages of the Pentagon Papers into the record of his subcommittee. This allowed the press and the public to see the real picture of what was occurring in Vietnam. All of these events, as well as the break-in of Richard Nixon's collaborators into the Democratic Party Headquarters at the Watergate Hotel, exerted enough pressure on him to disgracefully resign from the presidency. Then came the "honorable" withdrawal of the American forces in Vietnam in 1975, but which, in reality, was a humiliating defeat. We all saw on television the frantic scrambling for passage on helicopters atop the U.S. Embassy building as the United States Armed Forces evacuated Saigon. The degree of discord in this country over the Vietnam War had been horribly punctuated at Kent State University when students were fired upon by members of the Ohio State National Guard back in 1970 during a peaceful demonstration. We later learned that General Westmoreland and his commanders had falsified reports as to the status of the war so President Johnson could entertain a false sense of impending victory. It was later learned that Robert S. McNamara, the Secretary of Defense and the recognized architect of the Vietnam War, later admitted that going into Vietnam was a colossal mistake. And so, for the first time in U.S. history, a president was forced to resign in disgrace (1974) for obstructing justice involving a common burglary. And all the while, as we entered the early 1970s, we were laughing at the preposterous Bunker family that lived on Houser Street that put into some comic relief some of the important social issues of the day.

In June of 1978, the Jarvis-Gann Proposition 13 further eroded the financial support for the California public schools, which in the 1960s had been ranked nationally as among the best, but had fallen to 48th in many surveys of student achievement. Some have disputed Proposition 13's direct role in the move toward State financing of public schools because schools financed mostly by property taxes were declared unconstitutional in Serrano vs. Priest and Proposition 13 was then passed partially as a result of that case. California's spending per pupil was the same as the national average until about 1985 when it began dropping, which led to another referendum. Proposition 98 required a certain percentage of the State's budget to be directed towards education. It could be argued that all citizens of California and, indeed, the whole United State have a vested interest in educating its young and property taxes should be proportionally assessed to all land and property owners. It seems that the primary argument for the "People's Initiative to Limit Property Taxes" was that older Californians should not be priced out of their homes through high taxes. This could have been remedied by allowing a special exemption as they do in some states for the elderly and those living on modest incomes.

Even juvenile probation officers who had some leverage in the past to intercede with the incorrigible individuals lost that capacity due to the excessive liberalization of juvenile court laws passed in California in 1961. Children were entitled to be represented in juvenile court by their own-attorney— often in opposition to those of their own parents. Civil rights became such a priority issue that even the mentally incompetent were released from institutional care under the leadership of Governor Ronald Reagan (1967-1975) and put on the streets to fend for themselves, giving rise to a homeless phenomenon never before seen in this country.

The reluctance to address the problems forthrightly among our legislatures, judges, and parole boards had paved the way for unspeakable atrocities committed by violent felons who were freed to prowl the communities of law-abiding citizens and devastate their lives. The "new liberalism" had reduced government to a farcical drama without the will to assert itself in the interest of the common good. It had instigated rage among majorities and minorities as well. It bred a generation of poorly educated, poorly parented, and poorly inspired subcultures who would seek to waste their lives in hopelessness and drug addiction or to vent their rage and resentment in violent acts of vengeance and terrorism. Furthermore, the emergence of social discord and the resentment had seduced the legal profession in a way that subverts its integrity. Though the practice of law as a profession is inherently a noble social enterprise that seeks to ensure a sense of justice and fairness within the society, it has also attracted individuals with less noble character who, in the guise of nobility, have created further problems by generating excessive and greed inspired litigation. Because of excessive litigation, the medical profession felt compelled to practice what is called "defensive" medicine, which involved many procedures that were really unnecessary and very expensive. Likewise, there was also a reluctance of pharmaceutical to provide the new innovations of science and technology because they could be sued for enormous amounts of money if one of their products caused someone harm. The focus was not on the massive benefit, but on the harm that might occur to a very few. From a social point of view, it did appear that over the past 50 years there has been a diminution of community feeling and trust among the people and a loss of confidence in government systems and government officials, themselves, have become discouraged and disheartened. No longer can agreements be honored by a snake of hands as was the custom in the United

States for generations. Some of our best legislators have left government because they feel constantly frustrated to get important things done because the old comradeship of the Congress has been replaced by hostile partisanship and self-interest.

One of our most honored institutions, the U.S. Mail Service, which for generations had been a respected and dependable function of the government, has become inordinately expensive and often subject to poor morale. In past years, those who delivered the mail were held in high esteem for the responsibility and service they provided because every piece and letter was known to be important to the receiver but now it is so encumbered with "junk" and cheap advertising that its value has been diminished—while the price of a stamp keeps going up.

Women began asserting themselves and opting for equality with men in business and government. The concept of the "super mom" found a place in American jargon. Betty Friedan and Gloria Steinem led the Feminist movement and NOW (National Organization for Women) took extreme positions about the newly emerging role of women in America. Some advocated a complete independence from the domination of men on an equal basis. The new movement made stay-at-home mothers feel intimidated and diminished while others, like Phyllis Shlafley, espoused the more traditional activities of women such as motherhood, homemaking, and building character in their children while remaining the queen of the household. This revolution among

American women seemed to confuse and threaten men who were emotionally unequipped to deal with such changes. Men began to search for solutions in all-male sensitivity groups in order to understand the changing roles of women and to what extent they could assert themselves in this new context. As men became more sensitized towards women, women became more frustrated towards men. It became a very confusing arena of gender functions. This led to extreme reactions on both sides and laid the groundwork for such mating doctors as John Gray and his "Men Are From Mars, Women Are From Venus" books in order to lend some clarity to the issue and the whole nation teetered on the horns of this dilemma.

During the early '70s, about the time of Nixon's resignation in disgrace, OPEC (The Organization of Petroleum Exporting Countries) had decided to put the squeeze on the American oil industry by raising the price of their products (1973) and causing unbelievable gas lines on the streets of America. Petroleum intensive areas in the U.S. like Houston went into a severe economic depression and many had to leave the area and look for work elsewhere.

On September 17, 1978, a meeting was held at Camp David attended by the Egyptian President Anwar Sadat, Israeli Prime Minister Menachem Begin and U.S. President Jimmy Carter as an attempt to bring peace between Israel and Egypt following several military confrontations. A peace treaty was signed on March 26, 1979. In the Middle East, the goodwill initiative of Anwar Sadat of Egypt led to the Camp David Accords and set the stage for the remarkable developments toward peaceful coexistence between the Israeli and Arab factions—an ardent hope that, unfortunately, was never realized.

In 1982, there began a softening of relations between the Soviet Union and the United States as a result of a letter to the Premier Andropov written by a ten-year-old girl from Manchester, Maine by the name of Samantha Smith. She politely inquired, "If there could please be some way that she and her friends could grow up without the worry of a nuclear war." Because of her innocent and sincere letter, she was invited to spend two weeks in the Soviet Union among the children of that country. In a sense, she was the first female goodwill ambassador to the Soviet Union. This was the first softening of U.S./Soviet relations since WWII. Following this event, Gorbachev, who had been Andropov's protégé, assumed the leadership when Andropov died and that was beginning of the end of the Communist Soviet Union as we knew it.

By the end of the 1970s and into the '80's, people became more sensitized to the vulnerability of human life and it was during this time that a consciousness spread across the land having to do with safety, environmental protection, and life affirming health concerns. There were movements to clean up polluted lakes and rivers and toxic waste dumps, putting seat belts in automobiles and making cars more survivable, and paying attention to diet and exercise. Medical miracles were beginning to happen frequently. In foreign lands, Amnesty International and the concept of human rights became a significant movement and at home Greenpeace and The Sierra Club gave us a new appreciation of whales, dolphins, and all living creatures (and trees) great and small and at the same time a mysterious new virus among the homosexual community began making an appearance.

In 1979, our Embassy personnel were suddenly taken hostage in Iran following the defection of the U.S. supported Shah and the return of the Ayatollah Khomeini. Foreign policy had failed again. Interest rates skyrocketed further crippling the economy and public confidence. On the day of Ronald Reagan's swearing-in ceremony (1980) to the presidency, the hostages in Iran were released. It was later discovered that this came as a result of a clandestine arms deal carried out by undetermined agents and allowed Reagan "plausible denial" of any awareness of the matter. Later, an ambitious Marine Lt. Colonel by the name of Oliver North would appear prominently in other clandestine activities surrounding the Iran-Contra affair. The CIA was also found to be perpetrating sinister plots to overthrow the Sandinistas in Nicaragua. Communism was being cultivated in Central America and that was not tolerable except, of course, in Cuba. We had been burned there as a result of the Bay of Pigs fiasco during the Kennedy administration and after the Cuban Missile Crisis we decided that we had better peacefully coexist with Fidel Castro, hoping that with some mild embargos his own people would bring him down. Getting back to Reagan, the super optimist, super communicator, whose denial of the "deep pocket" tendencies of avaricious people and his supply side economics enabled opportunistic entrepreneurs to pad their pockets with over-extended government funding. Many short-term jobs were created erecting office space, which was never used. At the cost of government solvency, overextended credit provided enormous closing profits for the wheelers and dealers that probably set the stage for the hardships and "downsizing" of the '90s. in later years, plant closings, hostile mergers, and layoffs came to be a commonplace event. As a result of the excesses of the '80s and the fiscal irresponsibility of the Executive and Congressional Oversight Committees who looked the other way along with Reagan's tax cuts and crash arms race spending to break the back of the Soviets, we became the greatest debtor nation in the world; whereas, we had once been the greatest creditor nation on Earth. For some people it was a time to make hay and jump on the bandwagon of excess while plunging the nation into colossal debt and, at the same time, collapsing the old reliable Savings and Loan industry to the tune of $260 billion. It is true that this country enjoyed some years of prosperity and high morale, however, a glut of misguided arrogance eliminating interest rates and financial responsibility. Interest rates and financial responsibility culminated in the loss of the lives of American astronauts and a beloved teacher in the disaster of the Challenger space shuttle when the urgency to launch under very adverse conditions and for political aggrandizement resulted in a catastrophic failure for want of an "O" ring.

The enormous nuclear arms race and "wild west" showdown with the Soviets did appear to break the back of the already disintegrating Communist System. This event will probably go down in history as Reagan's greatest contribution, although the eight years of "Reaganomics" had tripled the national debt from $900 billion when he took office to more than a $2.8 trillion at the end of his term. At the same time, HIV infection became a frightening obsession because every day we learned of the skyrocketing escalation of this mysterious and fatal disease. All the while the AIDS epidemic began to jump to alarming proportions, excessive liberal persuasions provoked among homosexuals a wild and hysterical emergence from "the closet" and, at the same time, promoted aggressively a normalization and justification of the lifestyle to the public at large—and the AIDS epidemic rolled on. It became clear just how devastating this disease really was and never again would the word "gay" have the innocent and happy meaning as before. Even children now had to be introduced to the sordid facts of this terrible disease and its transmission. Childhood could no longer be a time of innocence and carefree exploration. It now became a time of wariness, hyper-vigilance, and premature prurient knowledge. Tragic stories of innocent children being afflicted by contaminated blood supplies were beginning to headline the news and some were advocating a testing of the entire population and a sequestration of those who had been found to be infected.

It was during the closing years of the 1980s that President George Herbert Walker Bush and his advisers gravely miscalculated the will and intentions of Saddam of Iraq that in turn led to the very destructive and costly "Desert Storm." During the Clinton administration that followed, the timidity and indecisiveness of the White House allowed for the butchery and mayhem to continue in Bosnia, Serbia, and Croatia from 1992 to 1995. And when the Clinton administration took over in 1992, complex divisions of interests emerged that further accentuated the political differences between a liberal Chief Executive and a conservative Congress; instead of resolving problems and making purposeful legislation, we got "gridlock" and mean-spirited antagonism. Issues that required the goodwill of the Congress, as well as the Executive branch, ranged from job creation and security, declining wages for workers (while enormous raises occurred in industry executive salaries bonuses), minimum wage issues, the role of gays and women in the military, universal and portable health insurance, Medicare, Medicaid, and Social Security, the moral questions, surrounding abortion, "workfare" funding and standards for education, and what to do about crime and drugs, and don't forget gun control. We had become, by far, the most violent nation in the world and guns were the weapon of choice. Other more technical/political issues emerged as to the line item veto, PAC campaign funding and the power of lobbyists in government, the feasibility of a third party, taxation unfairness and complexity, term limits, balancing the budget, reducing the size of the bloated federal government and returning more power to the States to solve their own social and economic problems, and not least, ethics. Since Watergate, the government seemed to have turned inward upon itself to present, at least outwardly, an image of self-purgation and impeccable morality; that is, until President Clinton's impeachment for sexual indiscretions in the Oval Office of the White House with Monica Lewinsky. Before he left the White House in 2001, President Clinton pardoned 100+ convicted felons whose offenses (U.S. Dept. of Justice) ranged from conspiracy, to drug trafficking, to tax evasion, to aiding and abetting, to forgery and perjury; an indiscriminate pardoning of criminals and setting of much more lenient standards for young people as to just what constitutes sexual behavior.

The great economic issues of the '90s came to be known as NAFTA and GAT (The North American Free Trade Agreement and the General Agreement on Trade), which some fear would further erode the standards of quality and excellence that had once been proudly shown on the label "Made in the U.S.A." Ross Perot had given convincing arguments to the effect that passage of these agreements would cause a "great sucking sound" as many of our industries would rush to other countries where cheap labor was abundant, further depleting our own labor force and standard of living. Cheaply produced commodities would flood the American market and cause American economic values to further decline. Our aggravating trade deficit with Japan in autos had embarrassed our own auto industry because they had let quality deteriorate and costs rise to where Americans were buying more Japanese vehicles. They were simply better. That kind of competition was healthy because it would seem that the market forces would motivate the American auto industry to wake up and produce a better product—-but it didn't. Our big industries were entrenched in their belief that nothing could effectively compete with American productivity. It would take a virtual collapse of the U.S. auto industry in 2008 and a bail out of enormous government funds to make major readjustments in how American industry viewed its true place in the economic realities of the 21st century. Most would agree that it is not in the interests of the United States to isolate itself from the rest of the world; however, it must enter into world trade agreements with some control and moderation. The U.S. ought not allow the standards of a third world nation to uncontrollably subvert those of our own country and yet we must be aware that there are emerging nations who are becoming more competitive due to an increased focus on education and a workforce that will work for cheaper wages.

As an explanation for all the unrest and disturbances in this society, many blame our violent culture, others our lack of religious training and taking religion out of the schools, others lament poor parenting and still others, political corruption and unworthy role models for the young. After all, we do see evidence of all this deterioration daily in our news broadcasts. We see children shooting other children in their classrooms and even crazed adults doing the same. In 1995 we all saw O.J. Simpson being acquitted of murdering his wife, Nicole Brown and her friend, Ronald Goldman as cameras were trained in on "White" and "Black" reactions to the verdict. The "Whites" couldn't believe it and the "Black" law students in Atlanta were overjoyed.

We see squabbles over whether or not to allow a judge to place the Ten Commandments in his court room. Parents seem desperate for answers to questions about how to raise their children and television shows attempt to bring on professionals of one stripe or another to answer such questions. It seems as our technology advances, our social maturity is falling behind. We see violence and poor sportsmanship in our high schools, our professional arenas, and even in parent supervised organized sports events for children. At the same time, ball players and entertainers are rewarded with enormous amounts of money while teachers and those whose responsibility it is to build a foundation for the future of this society in its young are barely rewarded with a living wage.

We would do well to reconsider the moral and ethical ideals that our forefathers diligently provided for us. They were based on the best acquired knowledge and wisdom of western civilization. We have been ignoring, it seems, the pearls of our heritage and instead have been groveling in the domain of our lower natures.

Instead of turning toward those baser forces and boldly confronting them, we have been turning away in the service of unrestrained accommodation and allowing the vulnerable young people of our society to become overwhelmed by the poison. William Pollack, Ph.D., in his book, "Real Boys," suggested that those who are most vulnerable will break down first. It is analogous to being susceptible to asthma and living in a polluted air environment. Dr. Pollack went on to say that in our society boys are trained to establish a "mask of masculinity" and to repress their tender or "feminine" feelings. Boys, therefore, cannot express sadness, loneliness or feelings of alienation without suffering ridicule from their peers and even from their parents in many cases. Only anger and aggressiveness are acceptable.

So in the pall and confusion of disjointed purposes, our government has been crippled and unable to resist the pressures of self interest groups and "victimized" minorities. We have become so fractionated in consensual purpose that we have become a society ruled by the self-centered goals of special interest group rather than "the rule of the majority" as was originally intended. Crisis reactions replaced long-term and thoughtful planning. In my view, in trying to please everyone, the government has become an unwieldy, overfed, effete organism and so the nation has become burdened with social disorder, cultural diffusion, colossal debt, and undisciplined spending.

As the new millennium approached, people were afraid that computers that had not been programmed properly would cause chaos and total disruption of financial transactions throughout the world. Fortunately, this did not happen and that anxiety was put to rest. Instead, as the new Bush administration took over the reins of government, the country was hit with a catastrophic event unseen since Pearl Harbor in 1941. On September 11, 2001, a hijacking of four American airliners by Islamic radical terrorists crashed into the World Trade Center and the Pentagon and flight 93 was heroically prevented from its intended target in Washington, DC by a few Americans who were unwilling to be commandeered by a few demented terrorists. Approximately 3,000 people were brutally and senselessly killed that day. In response to this tragedy, the Bush administration set out to exact justice in retaliation by dishonestly contriving a justification to attack Iraq on the alleged determination that Saddam Hussein was stockpiling nuclear weapons to be used against the U.S. It was later determined that there was no truth in this assumption. The inner circle of George W. Bush, Dick Cheney, Donald Rumsfeld, and David Addington executed a war with Iraq with no preplanning or circumspection as to how an occupation might be accomplished effectively. As it turned out, there was an insurgency uprising that would cost the lives of thousands of American soldiers and Iraqi civilians and set the stage for horrible episodes of torture.

For the next several years, there was to be a gross mismanagement of the occupation and a buildup of ill will against the U.S. throughout the world—and a loss of trust and faith in our own leadership and national purpose. Meanwhile, we became more embroiled in the Afghanistan situation and this opened up another war. That very sad thing that happened during this time was that the "No Child Left Behind" bill that was espoused by Bush during his early years in the White House was not financed as was intended in order for the Bush administration to finance the war in Iraq and Afghanistan—a congressional effort that would have had positive impact on the children of this country was sacrificed for Bush's unconstitutional war in the Middle East. The American people were once again told lies in order to justify and "unjust war" costing billions of dollars and a great number of American and Iraqi lives— and the consequent further decline in America's stature of moral leadership throughout the world.

George W. Bush was reelected for a second term over John Kerry of Massachusetts and New Orleans was hit with Katrina, a devastating and costly storm with great loss of human life and property. This all occurred because the banks and levees that protected the lower parishes were known to be incapable of withstanding excessively high wind and tides. Nothing was done about it by the Corp of Engineers who complained that they were simply not provided with sufficient federal funds to do the work. Before and after the devastation, the Bush administration proved to be unresponsive and ineffective in providing relief services. Where was the "compassionate conservatism" when it was needed?

Many abuses of corporate management began to emerge and the real estate market began feeling the effects of Greenspan's warning years ago about "irrational exuberance" and razzle-dazzle sub-prime mortgage loans and "creative financing" that allowed people to buy expensive homes as a speculation that the property would greatly increase in value and could be either refinanced (with anticipated equity) or sold at great profit. In the '80s and '90s, Wall Street came under the influence of a derivative debauchery of essentially "betting" on the market with greater and greater stakes. A warning was issued by Brooksley Born, a chairperson of the Commodity Futures Trading Commission (the federal agency that oversees the futures and commodity options markets of derivative abuses) of the consequent severe downturn in the economy but their warnings were ignored. During her tenure on the CFTC, Born lobbied Congress and President Clinton to give the CFTC oversight of off-exchange markets for derivatives in addition to its role with respect to exchange-traded derivatives. Her warnings were opposed by Federal Reserve Chairman, Alan Greenspan, along with Robert Robin and Lawrence Summers, whose economic philosophy followed that of Ronald Reagan and Ayn Rand in that "stay out of market regulation" and let the market regulate itself. It seemed that the country had been taken in by a pervasive sense of "getting it now" because for the present it seemed that America, as well as the world economy, was doing well. In recent times, Greenspan has admitted that he was wrong in his economic worldview and a recent ruling by the Supreme Court (in striking down corporate campaign spending limits) has again opened the way for further abuses of the system and to Brooksley Born is warning us again of that further downturns in the market until we learn from our experience.

In his book, "Free Lunch," David Johnston reminds us of some important issues pertaining to economic life in America:

- The power monger is no different from that of a cancer cell, which mindlessly seeks growth for the sake of its own self-interest until it overwhelms its host.
- After WWII our elected leaders worked to build and strengthen the middle class by investing in science, education, public health and medical research and infrastructures.
- In recent times we have turned away from these policies and government lobbying and special interests have allowed the growth and greedy to impose their will over the middle class and those least able to bear the burden thus subverting the foundations of this country.
- Other countries refer to their health systems as "health service" rather than "health insurance" as it is in this country. We do use a business model instead of a service model.
- Adam Smith tells us, "What improves the circumstances of the greater part can never be regarded as an inconveniency to the whole. No society can surely be flourishing and happy, of which the greater part of the members are poor and miserable."

- America ranks 36th among nations in its rate of infant mortality in 2006.
- President Bush said during the third election debate in 2004 that most of the tax cuts he sponsored went to low and middle income Americans. That was not even close to the truth. In fact, most of the savings—53%—went to people with incomes in the top 10% over the first 15 years of the cuts, which began in 2001 and would have to be reauthorized to keep them in effect through 2015. More than 15% of the tax cuts went to the top tenth of 1%, a group that is over 300,000 people.
- During Clinton's two terms he gave the richest of the superrich a much bigger tax cut than even Bush. Under Clinton, their effective tax rate fell by almost eight cents on the dollar, under Bush it fell only five.
- In terms of material well-being for children, the United Nations ranked the U.S. 17th on a list of 20 modern countries, right below Portugal.
- We now have almost three decades of experience with the idea that markets will solve our problems and the promises are not there. Many hundreds of billions of dollars have been diverted to the rich leaving our schools, parks, and local government services are starved for funds.
- We pour billion into subsidies for sports teams and golf courses, a folly Adam Smith railed against in his day. Our healthcare system cost us far more than that of any other industrial country and yet we live

shorter lives than Canadians, Europeans, and the Japanese.

As the 2008 election year came upon us, there was a strong feeling, it seems, among the people that we, as a nation, were heading in the wrong direction and real change was needed in order to set the Ship of State back on the right course. Ethics, morality, and trust in our society and government had been eroding for many years. We were sliding into what appeared to be a major recession or perhaps depression. Jobs began to disappear, unemployment started to rise to highs not seen since the early '30s and the U.S. auto industry started to hover on the edge of bankruptcy. The Arab-Israeli conflict continued to threaten the peace of the Middle East, and Iran posed a threat of developing a nuclear capability that would further destabilize the area. Pakistan, a nuclear power, presented itself as an unstable government and North Korea, again, appeared to be rattling sabers. Amidst all this, the American people elected a young man of African American-Moslem dissent, who campaigned on "change" and was so elected. He was a former president of the Harvard Law Review and a man of vision, leadership, and a will to restore American to its intended destiny.

After electing a "change" president, many Americans appear to be regretting the changes being implemented by the new president and what change at a much slower pace. Many are now espousing the need to move slowly because it does seem that when too many changes are made too rapidly and extreme movement is made in any direction there will be an opposing reaction—it seems to be a law of nature. The great philosophers taught moderation. Too much too soon of anything can lead to trouble and take us to places where "even angels fear to tread." This seems to be the major discontent with the current Obama administration. However our Ship of State has been far off course according to most and moving it back on course would have to entail a lot of discomfort and upheaval. It is questionable whether or not slow incremental degree changes will result in enough credible movement of provide a stimulus for further changes—particularly with the apparent impulse of our Congress to deadlock itself in oppositional, contentious, and partisan interests. Those politicians who have managed to ensconce themselves in their positions for many, many years seem to develop an investment to continue forming a web of personally advantageous networks. Knowing one's way around the "loop," so to speak, has its advantages, but also can defeat the purpose of good and responsible government. Perhaps if term limits for congressmen and senators could be established, as it is for the presidency, the return to the concept of the "citizen public servant" would help elected officials to stop basing their legislative choices on catering to the will of their well-heeled constituency for campaign money and truly consider the common good of the country as a whole. Furthermore, the influence of lobbying in legislature in order to influence heavily the special interests of those with persuasive financial power tends to defeat the interests of the "common good." Much needs to be done to restore the government to the will of the people rather than the will of a few. At the writing of this 2011 revision, it is the general consensus of the American people that our country is in a very dire situation with an enormous national debt that is rising beyond the capacity or will of our political leaders to control it, our very poor fiscal and monetary policies, the plunging real estate market, and very high unemployment. In addition, there does appear to be an over-bloating of personnel employed in the government sector and that needs to be trimmed down considerably.

There is also the impending threat that large corporations will not hire as before because much of what is produced can be done robotically and those jobs that will be available in the future will require a high degree of technical training and education, which our educational system is failing to accommodate. This country is becoming less competitive in these areas than China and India. It does, therefore, seem to suggest that a great focus must be put upon the sector of our economy that deals with small business and startup enterprises.

In a recent book published in 2011, the authors Weidemer, Weidemer, and Spitzer have written about what they describe as the "multibubble" economy that is threatening to collapse in two to five years and send the world into a massive economic "correction" that will create severe hardships. They are warning that we must be prepared because this is determined to happen. So what is a bubble economy? According to the aforementioned authors, "An economy that grows in a virtual upward spiral of multiple rising bubbles (real estate, stocks, private debt, dollar, and government debt) that interact to drive each other up, and that will inevitably fall in a vicious downward spiral as each following bubble puts downward pressure on the rest, eventually pulling the whole economy down." Their economic predictions have credibility because they had successfully predicted the downturn and recession of 2008.

CHAPTER SUMMARY

- After WWII, the U.S. was the dominant and victorious leader in the world and assumed responsibility for helping the defeated to regain economic and political stability through various aid programs. There was a sense that the U.S. had stood on high ground morally and ethically by saving Western civilization from another "dark age."

- Now, with the most powerful weapon on earth (the atomic bomb) the U.S. believed it could maintain the peace by stemming the nemesis of the world—Soviet communism. This led to the U.S. involvement in the Korean "peace action" through the United Nations compact—and, later, to the initial technical assistance program in Vietnam under John F. Kennedy. Due to the instability of the Vietnam government and Kennedy's instructions to unseat Diem as an instigator of religious antagonisms between Catholics and

Buddhists, we were headed for a disastrous outcome through military intrusion into affairs of foreign nations.

- Since our greatest adversary, the Soviet Union, had gained access to the nuclear bomb, the world became threatened by mutual destruction and more money had to be diverted from education to national defense. American society began a major change in reactionto the war mentality and gave risk to be "peacenik" movement and the escapism into drugs and "free love."

- Great feuding began occurring between the "Hawks and the Doves" and, at the same time, the African-American population clamored for recognition as being able to enjoy first-class citizenship under the Civil Rights legislation. Many were sacrificed on the altar of freedom, including President John F. Kennedy and the leader of the civil rights movement, Martin Luther King Jr., through assassination. Education became a back burner issue amid all the strife and discontent. Hasty and ill-conceived legislation and court imposed mandates created more discord and disarray among those in the school systems. Bifurcated attitudes prevailed regarding war and peace and human rights issues came to the forefront of public interest.

- The Jarvis-Gann legislation of 1978 further crippled school funding and stability and educational excellence continued in decline. People were feeling their taxes were stretched to the limit and further withdrew support to the schools. Tenure protected the week and burnt out while, at the same time, diminished the ranks of the newly trained, energetic, enthusiastic, and creative young people eager to enter the profession of teaching. Funding for schools took a backseat as more demands for financial resources to support out involvement in the Middle East, the Far East, our weapon race with the Soviet Union and a few minor military excursions in Cuba, Nicaragua, Panama, and Granada.

- "White-Black" issues jumped to the front pages of the Network news and were intensified by attempts to redress the wrongs of the past "affirmative action" and separate but lower standards of admission to colleges and universities. Animosity appeared to grow as "blacks" felt more and more that they were being classed as inferior and incompetent while being administered to in a patronizing way. Martin Luther's plea that "people be judged by the content of their characters rather than by the color of their skin" fell on deaf ears. The homosexual communities also had their grievances by feeling shut out of the mainstream of American society and the AIDS epidemic reached alarming heights.

- War in the Middle East and Wall Street greed set the stage for an oncoming economic crisis that was tantamount to the "Great Depression" of the 1930s and people were

not at all interested in "throwing money at the school systems."
- What is a "bubble economy?"

REVIEW QUESTIONS

- Do you think the U.S. had the moral responsibility to engage in military interventions in the Far East?
- Why do you suppose the Korean War was first referred to as a "police action?"
- How do you think our initial involvement in Vietnam as a "technical advisory" capacity expanded to the extent that it did?
- What you understand by the phrase "Hawks and doves" with reference to our foreign policy?
- What were the "peaceniks?"
- Do you think the racial issues of the '60s could've been handled more effectively?—- "Affirmative Action," etc.
- Describe how the Jarvis-Gann legislation interfered with school funding and stability.
- Do you think our military involvement in foreign affairs after WWII can be justified?
- Do you think it was a good thing to go to war in Iraq and Afghanistan and why?
- Do you think big business interests ought to be given free reign on the market without government oversight and control?
- How can you explain how the U.S. economy became so critical?

PART II

Reforming a New America

At this time, in the summer of 2012, the U.S. is coming to another "crossing of the Rubicon" and it is believed that history from now on will mark this period as the sad demise of a great and promising a new Republic or the beginning of an innovative and re-creative new adventure in hopeful and purposeful living.

In his book, "Come Home, America,. The Rise and Fall (And Redeeming Promise) of Our Country," William Greider quotes Adam Smith, founder of modern market economics, who was on the side of compassion. Greider goes on to say that Smith was revered by Economists for describing "the invisible hand" of the marketplace and taught that "moral sentiments"—human acts of "fellow feeling"—are the guiding forces that govern economics and prevent markets from injuring society. He further describes that empathy for others, self-interested mutuality, and other moral verities—are the things that Adam Smith taught (and most modern economists ignore).

For many years now government and private corporations have been ignoring these ideals of our early American history and collaborating to skew our society in the direction of a bifurcated populace of the extremely wealthy and the extremely impoverished. According to author Holly Sklar, the average wage for full-time workers in 1982 was $34,199.00 in comparison (buying power) with 2006 dollars. In 2007, twenty-five years later, the average wage for full-time workers was $34,861.00.

On the other hand, in 1982 when Forbes magazine first published its annual list of the four hundred richest Americans, there were only thirteen billionaires among them. Twenty-five years later, the Forbes 400 consisted entirely of billionaires and eighty-two were left off the 2007 list because they were not rich enough to make the cut. This great divergence of wealth is why families have had to take on extraordinary levels of debt as they try to stay afloat and keep up with mortgage payments when their incomes are no longer rising. In 2005, US household savings went negative—people spent more than they earned—for the first time since 1933.

Since Barack Obama was elected in 2008, his administration has been dedicated to restoring a balance between conservative and liberal persuasions, but the Republican Party from the start has cast accusations that he is moving the country toward Socialism and they have opposed every significant bill advanced by President Obama or the Democratic majority. However, these criticisms dissolve under the most rudimentary examination of the facts. Firstly, Sam Tanenhaus, in his recent book, "The Death of Conservatism," has stated that the decision of Obama's team to fortify the banking system and improve the flow of credit is, unequivocally, an attempt to salvage the free market. Fearful allegations that bailing out GM would result in nationalizing the auto industry had proven false. Secondly, Obama's plan to extend health coverage to the nearly fifty million Americans who lack it is no more socialistic that providing Medicare for citizens over the age of 65. In Obama's first year, it was no longer enough to oppose the Obama's health-care reform bill. They warned that it was federal "take-over" and Speaker of the House, John Boehner, recently commented that the entire Obama health care law ought to be "taken out by the roots." At a town-hall meeting, Bob Inglis, a House Republican from South Carolina, was besieged by angry constituents. One said, "Keep your hands off my Medicare." Inglis replied, "Actually, sir, your health care is being provided by the government." And thirdly, Obama's foreign policy premised on diplomacy and multilateral concord, is as forceful a repudiation of the imperial presidency as we have seen in the modern era.

All these are the actions of a leader who, while politically liberal, is temperamentally conservative and who has placed his faith in the durability—and renewability—of American institutions.

Another example of the oppositional attitude of the Republicans in the Congress, it should be pointed out, is that in 2009 the Republicans objected that the Obama stimulus plan offered too little help to small businesses. But when Obama, conceding the point, proposed an infusion of $30 billion to those businesses, with the sum drawn from TARP (troubled asset relief program) funds, Republicans instantly ridiculed the plan for no apparent reason other than to deny Obama a victory. The message of the Republicans is sheer stridency and opposition. Accusations that Obama is a covert socialist were made by Newt Gingrich and Rush Limbaugh in the Conservative Political Action Conference in February of 2009. When the group reconvened the following year, it was Glenn Beck who summarized the latest version of the movement by saying that,"Progressivism is the cancer in America." He went on to say that the Democrats were "liberal neomonarchists" and "would kill the very spirit that has built the nation." Where are the reasonable conservatives today? Robert Taft believed in taking a stance of opposition and criticism although he supported Social Security and public housing and— overcoming his isolationist principles—approved both NATO and the Marshall Plan.

There is so much dissention today in our Congress with so little meaningful legislation. It is almost as though most Americans are resigned to an ever declining Nation with little hope of a resurgence of spirit and optimism. There is an oft quoted analogy of the frog that jumps into a pot of water. The frog is unaware that the temperature of the water is gradually rising and he adapts to the increasing heat until he suddenly realizes that the heat will kill him if he doesn't get out but by this time he is so weak he doesn't have the strength to save himself. I don't think this analogy holds up for Americans because any society of people who could summon the energy and communal effort, almost overnight, as they did during WWII to meet the challenge of survival can summon, again, the will and determination to capture the wind and set the luffing Ship of State on its intended course.

The following are a few ideas gleaned from many sources mentioned in the "Reading Material" list at the end of this essay:

"Only a single payer system of national health care can save what we estimated is the $350 billion wasted annually on medical bureaucracy and redirect those funds to expand coverage," Himmelstein and Woodhandler wrote in the New York Times.

Other nations have demonstrated that a nationalized system put a lid on prices and profits, the main source of the perennial inflation of health care costs. The U.S. approach, in contrast to other successful health care systems, rewards the private sector and punishes the customers. The adversaries, to this concept of health service rather than health insurance, object because they think it is "socialistic." This is a gross distortion of reality by catastrophizing systems that provide services and supports for all the people without disturbing the entrepreneurship of those who stimulate the industry and business of the country. Admittedly, the initial cost of a conversion would be considerable, but less than Washington quickly spent on rescuing Wall Street firms. An estimated saving would be $30 billion a year. It is interesting to note that during WWII and by 1946 the accumulated government debt had reached 120% of the GDP. Many people thought the nation would collapse under the weight of its debt and feared it would slide back into a depression. However, the opposite turned out to be true. After the war, the post-war economy expanded greatly and launched the most successful recovery the world had ever seen. This was accomplished, in large part, by all the investment in new factories and new technologies and instituting the "socialistic" GI Bill that allowed returning veterans to go to college and support the emergence of a stronger middle class. So, as WWII demonstrated, the reality test is not the size of the federal budget but whether the borrowed money is invested for the future.

The pension system is in very poor working order. This nation lives with an extraordinary contradiction. In an era when financial wealth has grown explosively, millions of baby boomers now find themselves approaching retirement with paltry savings and no pensions. They will have to keep working into their old age or accept a sharp drop in their standard of living. Social Security, the bedrock insurance for the elderly, provides income equivalent to the federal minimum wage. The old-style corporate pensions that guaranteed retirement benefits are fast disappearing as companies shed them to boost their profits. However, we can look to the many successful models. The Pension Rights

Center proposes doing a lot of readjusting of the 401 (K) system. A proposal was made for a new and inclusive national pension that alongside Social Security would require all employees to save in exchange for guaranteed portable individual pension accounts that would pay up to 70% of preretirement earning. Furthermore, there are many successful models that use this approach and provide stable, reliable retirement benefits, including low-overhead, non-profit administrators with no game playing and no profiteering. Examples, include mandatory TIAA-CREF pensions for college professors, the construction trades, multiemployer pension plans jointly managed by labor and management, foreign systems like Australia's new national pension system, and the U.S. government's own Thrift Savings Plan for federal employees.

Restoring just taxation is a moral cause, but also a major step toward financing big changes in the society. A direct tax on wealth is considered unacceptable in American politics because it is said it amounts to "confiscation" of private property. However, homeowners pay a "wealth tax" every year at the local and state levels—the property tax on their homes—and no one calls it confiscatory. The largest wealth holders and financial institutions could be offered a choice—either pay a modest wealth tax to the government or invest the equivalent in a list of innovative priority ventures or public improvements. There are so many ways to make significant changes and improvements in American political society and we must ask ourselves if the status quo is really what we want for the future of our country. The point is that the nation must mobilize capital to undertake hundreds or thousands of large-scale, long-term projects to bring the unemployment rate down, provide substantial jobs and invest in the future with structural reconstruction.

Many people strongly objected to FDR's administration because they thought he seized too much executive power and with all his projects was moving the country toward socialism. The fact is that his administration set the stage for a victory over the Axis powers during World War II and substantial economic recovery after the war. FDR enumerated a list of "rights" that would for many years be the textbook for political reform and social advancement. They included the following:

- The right to a useful and remunerative job;
- The right to earn enough to provide adequate food, clothing, recreation and medical care;
- Freedom (for businesses) from unfair competition and domination by monopolies;
- The right to adequate protection from the economic fears of old age, sickness, accident and unemployment;

It was not believed that our forefathers intended America to manage the world. That is not why people from all over came to America. They came to be free of tyranny and oppression and the freedom to practice their better intentions and make a better life for themselves and their children. Unfortunately, the dark side of our heritage also manifested a mistreatment and brutality in the form of indentured slavery of African, Chinese and Hispanic people and American Indians. With regard to these groups, their full civil and social respect has been a long and difficult struggle but there has been progress. As someone once said, "it's not so much in reaching the end of a journey but knowing you are heading in the right direction."

One could say that our global posture since the late '50s has been undermining what made this nation strong, including those constitutional principles that have been corrupted in U.S. efforts to prevail aggressively throughout the world. On the contrary, turning inward will actually make it easier for the United States to work out new relations with the other countries. Instead of dominating others, we can learn to live with differences. Instead of attacking foreign governments that deviate from the U.S. model, America can once again serve as a model of self-determination for all nations. In 1958, William J. Lederer gave us a heads up lesson in American arrogance by writing his book, "The Ugly American," which showed how an overbearing foreign policy led to grave errors of judgment and foreign relations in Southeast Asia that we do not want to repeat again. Perhaps, aggression with guns and tanks and planes will give way to wars with cyberspace and technical intelligence. This means that our young people must be educated to meet challenges.

In the last few decades, the U.S. economy has drifted further from the promises of the compassionate administrations, creating in its place a broad labor market of the underclass-temporary jobs paying unlivable wages and often filled with illegal immigrants. Guaranteed public jobs paying more than the minimum wage would permanently and automatically stabilize the economy, swelling the ranks of public workers in recessions and shrinking them when private jobs became abundant. Instead of punishing the working poor most severely in downturns, as the system now does, it would redistribute the costs to all taxpayers to share as a public obligation. Real jobs would mean that reliable incomes would flow into those underprivileged communities, providing a concrete basis for economic development and neighborhood restoration as well as the redemption of damaged lives. If the job slots included school-age young people and men and women in the bleakest circumstances they could suddenly become valued members of their families and the communities in which they would go to work producing real improvements while gaining for themselves a foothold on the economic ladder. If eligibility were linked to continuing their education, young people would get practical on-the-job training and a strong reason to stay in school. Even the American military could provide expertise in training young people. Old sergeants know how to take unpromising kids and turn them into highly competent and disciplined young people.

Starting in the 1920s, there was philosophy of that era, improbable as it sounds today, that was known as corporate liberalism. General Electric was the leading exponent of the progressive-minded companies. Greider points out that during the 1920s, GE was a pioneer in developing workplace and community relations that defused the harsher conflicts of labor vs capital. Before government became a social activist, General Electric was already experimenting with innovations like profit sharing and worker councils. Its CEO even articulated a vision that someday workers would become the company's owners as the majority shareholders. Cooperation, GE argued then, enhances efficiency and sustains profit and long-term prosperity. Other big names like Kodak, DuPont, General Motors, U.S. Steel and Standard Oil also supported various progressive measures. Collectively, would provide their employees with job security; industrial wages that rose in step with productivity; and health insurance, pensions, and other benefits, and inclusive bargaining would be the means to settling disputes. Not everyone in the country benefited, but the industrial arrangement became the core model for the postwar economy and helped create the large and stable American middle class.

The concept of "corporate liberalism" that was prominent in the 1920s with some of the great corporations was to reconsider the employee morale by insuring that everyone who works, whether in management or on the assembly line, deserved to "own" their work, i.e. to exercise personal responsibility for what they do and enjoy the mutual respect and the right to contribute and collaborate in making important decisions and share in the profits. These elements of voice and status are very important to personal satisfaction in one's work. The most progressive companies encourage the cooperative spirit from top to bottom. Most people take a great deal more care and responsibility when they have investment of ownership and that also applies to one's work. Numerous academic studies have shown and outstanding companies already understand that collaborative relationships between top management and the workforce are more productive and profitable. The profits are shared because the workers are also the owners.

Our history of unions in this country goes back to the 1800s and the Industrial Revolution when workers were highly exploited, giving rise to a more aggressive movement to unionize workers for their protection and decent treatment. The concept of labor-management relations had roots going back to the Protocol of Peace by Louis Brandeis in 1912 followed by the New York City garment workers' strike that same year. Later, in 1949 Dorothea de Scheinitz published her work on labor and management in a common effort to reach cooperative understandings.

Unfortunately, in the 1970s it all fell apart. Major companies began to break the truce with organized labor (largely due to the aggressive stand of Ronald Reagan regarding the Air Traffic Control Patco Union issue) and also turned hard against the government. The business Roundtable and other groups, allied with hard-right ideologues, were taking command of the Republican Party. General Electric once again led the way, this time as the premier example of the harsh new bottom-line strategy that put corporations in conflict with workers and social values. Frank P. Doyle, GE executive vice president, acknowledged in retirement, "We did a lot of violence to the expectations of the American workforce." At that point, liberal Democrats might have reformed the regulatory system to make it more flexible. Instead, they retreated with the election of Ronald Reagan in 1980 and the old liberal order was over.

One of the dominant themes of the decades from the 1920s up through the 1970s had been the reversal of the historic role of unions, namely, steadily increasing wages and benefits in order to share in the company's driven by union had been made possible through comparable increases in productivity and the result was an overall reduction of inequality in society. Then starting in the early 1980s, an adversarial stance was taken by management to retrieve distributive gains that had been won by unions and their members over the years. Management used forcing and threatening strategies and was often prepared to use the threat of bankruptcy to gain the advantage. About that time, according to Daniel Di Salvo, assistant professor of political science at the City College of New York, wrote, "Government-workers" unions have been political juggernauts in the U.S. since the unseen collective-bargaining-rights revolution of the 1960s and '70s. These unions are different and more powerful than those of bottle owners and managers in the private sector. To advance their interests, unions in the public sector have created cartels with their political allies, mostly in the Democratic Party, to the exclusion of the taxpaying public." In Daniel Di Salvo's book, "Government Union and the Bankrupting of America," he gives an excellent outline of how this aspect of a government takeover of public service happened and that can be done to protect the public interest.

On the private sector side, as we all know, corporations started to outsource factories and services and jobs to foreign countries thereby lowering their cost of labor. At the same time, management and higher positions in the corporations began giving themselves huge salaries, bonuses and "golden parachute" severances from the company. In the meantime, as mentioned at the beginning of this essay, the buying power of worker wages had not significantly improved over the last 25 years. On a more cynical note, one might think of what has been happening as the "rape of America."

A full scale effort on the part of both private and public agencies must be waged through the willingness to invest in the future by creating the many jobs needed to reinforce our dilapidating infrastructure. As pointed out before, the vast investments made during WWII gave rise to the great economic recovery and sustained stability for many years. This must be accompanied by standards of equitable and cooperative participation in the direction, productivity and profits of our corporations.

One other concern of many Americans today in our modern society is the issue of Islamic immigration. There have been books written about the "Infiltration" of seditious Islamic forces threatening our national security. I have heard and read reports that Europe and Western Civilization that was founded on Judeo-Christian religious principles are giving way to Muslim influences and Sharia law even though demographic studies show that France and Germany have the largest proportion of Muslims and that amounts to only seven and eight percent, respectively. It appears that there are concentrations of these cultural/religious groups much like other ethnic groups have formed in our own country. It is not unusual until generations that follow become assimilated and enculturated into the larger society. It is unreasonable, in my view, that a host nation would simply take a "live and let live" attitude while neglecting the establishment of social boundaries. In other words it ought to be established that those who have come as immigrants respect the laws and culture of the host country. When Americans go to live in an Arab country it is expected that the Americans must respect the laws and customs of that country. It is only courtesy if nothing else.

These are divisions among the Islamic people-the Shia and the Sunni sects. In terms of leadership, the Shia hold that leadership must come by inheritance directly from Mohammed while the Sunni, which represent 85% of the Islam population, take the position that leadership must be earned by proving oneself worthy and capable. These bifurcations are not uncommon. When you look at traditional Roman and Byzantine Catholic and then Roman Catholic and Protestant-Jewish Orthodox and Jewish Reform, even political divisions of reactionary conservative and radical liberal, there is an obvious tendency on the part of human nature to want to stay close to the familiar and traditional, on the one hand, and the desire to move forward on the other. There have been militant elements in Judeo/Christianity as in the Crusades and the Inquisition which was sanctioned and bloody seekers of martyrdom. My sense is that in Islam, the militancy movement is on a much smaller scale than was the barbarism of the early Church. I am not persuaded that Islamic leadership is dedicated to the destruction of Western Civilization although there are elements that do—just as early Christianity sought to Christianize the world. Perhaps, Islam, being a younger religion, is also going through stages of evolution that Christianity has gone through. Reza Aslan, in his book, "No god but God" points out how different sects have interpretations that are demeaning and punitive while another is more considerate and respectful. In another book by Irshad Manji titled, "The Trouble with Islam Today," she is urging those of her religion to reform the faith, empower women, encourage independent thinking and respect for the views of others.

So where are the roots of our political woes? In my view, the fate of our future lies in the quality of parent/child relationships and good learning experiences. Those of us who have studied Political Science and History as well as Psychology can see that if a child is treated kindly and with respect of his own personhood as he/she is growing up, that person will feel good about themselves and be inclined to move forward into the world with confidence and good will while, on the other hand, if the child grows up without positive regard or is an object of abuse of one kind or another, that child is likely to carry over its perception of the world as hostile and unfriendly and must, in adulthood, elect to take on the extraordinary challenges and struggles to correct faulty learning and experience or become an incompetent liability to others. In the latter situation, the child who does not feel good about him or herself will likely either turn against the self or others in some malignant way—and, in either case, that person will likely become a wasted human resource and be costly to the world at large. Our prisons and psychiatric wards are glutted with such individuals—not to mention those who plague the world with colossal exploitations. When seen on a scale of extremes, we can note the brutal, exploitive, narcissistic bully or the self-defeating unproductive and unhappy recluse on the one hand or the cooperative, friendly and contributing member of society who raises healthy, happy and productive children on the other. On a lesser scale of extremism we can see those of a political persuasion who favor or perhaps need to stay on familiar ground toward the traditions of the past or those who are more emboldened to seek new adventures and knowledge. The social, economic, and political community, therefore, must be capable of providing a government that enables all people within that society the security it needs in order to pursue its better intentions.

To conclude this essay I would like to present a few more ideas toward a reformation of our political-economic society:

We, the Friends of the Republic say:

1. The Federal Reserve Central bank has not been working in our best interests and should be abolished and that private banks, with some competent State oversight, would better serve the people.
2. In the future large corporations, or small ones for that matter, should be held responsible for the consequences of their failures, either intentional or unintentional. We all have to learn from our mistakes.
3. The Federal government ought to be reduced to only the functions of national defense, inter-state commerce and social security. Furthermore, if all the functions and bureaucracies were kept at the State level, there would likely be enough to provide free education up through the university level and free medical services for all the citizens of the State as well as enough funds to provide for those unable to care for themselves. This is necessary to insure a viable and self-enhancing society.
4. There ought to be standards of social conscience and professional competence established for anyone who aspires to serve in public office. A Democratic Republic is a wonderful form of government but it does have its limitations if the quality and character of the leadership is wanting.

5. There must be penalties for anyone who does not exercise their civic responsibility and cast their vote. When we see what people in less fortunate countries do to make sure their votes are recognized, it makes us feel rather dismayed at the lack of enthusiasm of our own people.

6. The executive branch of the government has become so over-burdened with gigantic responsibilities and complexities that we ought to consider having two Chief Executive; one for foreign affairs who has some expertise and demonstrated competencies and understanding of those kinds of responsibilities and one for domestic affairs with proven expertise in their respective fields. In addition, we might have a Board of individuals at the top who are chosen to represent the character and integrity of this country's ideals of honesty, fair play and good sportsmanship. The ethics and moral standards of our country in business and industry have been so dissimulated that our children hardly know what this nation stands for anymore.

7. Our leaders could become a bit more humble and circumspect so that we might learn from those in other countries who have done better than we in such areas as medical services. In an interview on the Fareed Zacaria program, a guest who had studied medical services around the world had discovered that Switzerland has had a health service system very similar to what is called "Obama Care" for the past 18 years and it is working beautifully for virtually all the

people and at a much lower cost than ours. They call their system a medical service. We call ours medical insurance and that is because it is a competitive industry and much more expensive. It, therefore, must serve the financial interests of the share and stockholders.

8. Lobbyists in Washington wield too much influence on the Congress and serve only the purposes of the large corporations. They are able to spend a great deal more money than most of us have to spend in fortification of their own special interests. This puts a great disadvantage over those of the middle class— the backbone of America—and those who have been elected by the people to represent them in a fair and equitable manner.

9. The income tax issue is a vexing one and offends those of us who must pay large amounts of money to someone else to figure out how much we must pay the government because it has become much too complicated for even those of us who are well educated professional people to do ourselves. Frankly, it's an abomination and must be returned to something simple as it was in years past.

10. One of the major keystones of any healthy, progressive and competitive society is education. In terms of priorities, it should come before sports and entertainment because of its ultimate value in preserving and advancing the viability of future generations of Americans. Education should not be politicized or bureaucratized, but regarded as a true profession and those that enter it ought

to be so regarded with standards of excellence the norm.

11. Our country is suffering from a lack of talented and capable leadership because of the extraordinary amount of money it takes to run for political office. It favors only a few who have large funds of money and are supported by those with large sums of financial resources. Furthermore, running for another term detracts from the time and energy an elected official ought to be spending at his job. I'm not sure what a better answer would be, but it does seem to us that the broadcasting companies ought to be prevailed upon to donate some air time to a worthy prospective aspirant for public office since they are supported by sponsors that gain from the public consumer.

12. In view of the fact that people are living much longer than they were when Social Security was established, it would be better for all of us if the retirement age were boosted up to 70 with early retirement an option at 68. Furthermore, part-time continued employment could be established as a normal pattern and that would allow those who have gained so much experience and skill in particular occupations to pass on to younger employees and those newly entering the market place the benefit of what the elder people have learned. Another consideration is the fact that much of production and services are being provided by workers overseas, robotics and home office employment. It seems feasible, therefore, that the work hours be shortened so

people can have more time to enjoy their families and for recreation.

13. The issue of gun control in the U.S. is one of grave importance. According to Wikipedia sources (in the year 2000), there were 52,447 deaths deliberately caused by firearms and 23, 237 accidental deaths caused by firearms. According to the CDC/National Center for injury prevention and control, the U.S. death rate from firearms in 2003 was eight times higher than its counterparts in other parts of the world. We ought to realize that when this issue was considered by framers of our Constitution, people lived in outlying and isolated farms and were vulnerable to attacks from outlaws, Indians, wild animals and even British sympathizers. It made sense for people who lived in those times to have some way of defending themselves. Today, however, we live in a civilized society protected by police forces and legal prohibitions—at least this is what is intended. We must take firearms (and especially those that are intended for war) out of the hands of those who are incapable of handling them responsibly—or at least, as Senator Moynihan once said in 1993, if we can't control guns, at least let us tax bullets and ammunition or set standards on who is allowed to purchase them. The other alternative, as suggested by John R. Lott, Jr. in his 1998 publication "More Guns-Less Crime," is to legally allow all citizens to carry firearms as a protection against those who would be a threat.

14. Finally, the beauty of our system is that our forefathers understood that nothing is perfect so they designed our form of government to be changeable and improvable as the knowledge and awareness of the people evolves and grows. It is based on the premise that reasonable people of goodwill can sit down together with differing views and persuasions and talk sensibly about a consensual course of action for the betterment of all. With the sincere input of the leaders, one can determine which confluence of ideas will likely give the best results for the needed choices and directions.

In addition, we do not want to omit the wise recommendations of Warren Buffet who, in a recent interview with CNBC, offered persuasive reform measures in his Congressional Reform Act of 2012 as follows:

1. No tenure/no pension: Congress men and women collect a salary while in office and receive no pay when they are out of office.
2. Congress (past, present & future) participates in Social Security: All funds in the Congressional retirement fund move to the Social Security system immediately. All future funds flow into the Social Security system, and Congress participates with the American people. It may not be used for any other purpose.
3. Congress can purchase their retirement plan, just as all Americans do.

4. Congress will no longer vote themselves a pay raise. Congressional pay will rise by the lower of CPI or 3%.
5. Congress will lose their current health care system. They must participate in the same health care systems as the American people.
6. Congress must equally abide by all laws they impose on the American people.
7. All contracts with past and present Congressmen and women are void effective 12/1/12. The American people did not make these contracts with Congressmen or women. Congress made all these contracts with themselves.

Serving in Congress is an honor, not a career. The Founding Fathers envisioned citizen legislators, so ours should serve their term (s), then go home and back to work.

Isn't it time we cleaned house and thought about new guidelines for our country's future? Let's all the express our thoughts and feelings to the politicians in Washington and let them know the will of the people.

CHAPTER 3

The whole question of what constitutes an effective and viable educational and social milieu and what promotes a truly nurturing community has evoked great interest in recent years among many thoughtful people. The immediate future is fraught with towering social, political, and economic problems such as environmental preservation and conservation of natural resources, including air and water, population management, crime, social disorder, international political and trade relations, infrastructure, transportation, and circulation problems in our large cities, urban blight, health care, and an economy that thrives and provides not only jobs, but interesting and challenging jobs with a constantly improving standard of living. The implications, therefore, for the professional educator is to teach and train young Americans in a way that enables them to cope creatively and productively with all those problems and challenges with faith and confidence in American life. Young people must be taught to value the long-range implications of their endeavors rather than the myopic and short-term crisis oriented view of immediate self-interest and instant gratification.

Perhaps a new direction in educational thought might be a creative and penetrating search for viable goals and values, old and new, rather than a perpetuation of the bureaucratic, factory model of education that served us well in times past. Now we need a search that leads toward an understanding of inner reality and an appreciation of individual differences, perceptions, and divergent cultures. It can be paid for the value you render and the American purpose can be thought of as the continuing opportunity to pursue one's own destiny while being supported in a humanized community and social structure. In any case, effective education is a multi-dimensional experience involving not only the teacher and the student, but the home and community as well.

So, what can be done about it? What can the American people do to set the Ship of State on a course toward greater purpose and as a beacon to the rest of the world? Much needs to be done in many areas of endeavor such as: all levels of government, business and industry, and the banks and financial institutions, to name a few; however, it is the intention of this book to stress the need for educational reform and in that regard that I submit the following suggestions:

- *The Grading System*: The A to F traditional grading system has within it the demeaning evaluation of assigning the C grade to most of the students in a class thereby designating most to a status of mediocrity while others are either evaluated as successful or unsuccessful depending on whether you are given an A or B or a D or an F. The point is that in the early stages of a child's development such a grading system will likely influence his/her self-concept in a way as to lock in a mindset of mediocrity or incompetence. Young kids are always very impressionable and influenced by external evaluations until they are older and have had enough experience of themselves to discern their own capacities. One might say, what about building a healthy sense of competition? Competition is highly valued in America, but it seems to me that it ought to be a chosen option at a later age rather than an enforced one in the primary years. If the student learns to interpret his/her worth and capacities from early competitive evaluations of mediocre conformity or incompetence by the imposition of an enforced grading system, he might very well generalize his sense of competency in other areas of life as well. I have known of very young children being psychologically damaged because they "flunked" first grade and had to be kept behind their classmates. Several years ago William Glasser, in his book, "School Without Failure," suggested that young children be allowed to approach the problem of learning somewhat at their own pace and readiness, but within a continuous group with frequent evaluations of performance as to pass, superior, or incomplete. The point being that students must learn to internalize standards for achievement, excellence, and success in order to build self-knowledge, self-acceptance and motivation. What some see as a better option is to have a completely un-graded and continuous small grouping of young students from the time they enter school until having completed four years with highly intensive instruction in the basics so that they may all enter fourth grade with the skills and knowledge to proceed with success. An effective screening upon entering school will uncover any special problems that require remediation and support can also be given to enlist the parents in ways that can enrich and encourage their children's motivation. It all has to do with mental attitude. (See Appendix VI.)

- *Individual Styles of Learning*: Each student must be acknowledged to be the unique individual that he/she is with their own style of learning. We know that children are endowed with capacities for varying levels and qualities of learning and abstraction; i.e. intuitiveness as opposed to the "hands on" approach, problem solving through thoughtfulness and ideas rather than the quality of feeling and social energy, seeing the world perceptively rather than in the sense of structure and closure. These individual differences can be observed early in the child's development (and objectively described in such assessment instruments as the Myers-Briggs Type Indicator). This seems hardly possible when the competition for rewards and privileges stem from a frantic preoccupation with comparing oneself with the achievements of others. If competition for the rewards of successful learning are first related to personal achievement as a chosen option rather than as an imposed one then we are strengthening self-awareness and a greater degree of inner-directedness. To experience oneself as a failure at an early impressionable stage of development because of self-doubt instead of autonomy and incompetence, or inferiority instead of industry as described by Erik Erikson, is to set the stage for frustration, discouragement and hopelessness. The juvenile court authorities acknowledge that such negative attitudes lead to alienation, resentment and anti-social disposition.

- *Interest and Motivation*: The movement toward individualization of instruction (which now occurs almost exclusively in the special education of the learning handicapped) places an emphasis upon the teaching of highly relevant and stylized material with a view toward stimulating and motivating the student along with frequent evaluations of progress so the student can have the kind of feed-back that builds confidence. It is interesting to note the degree of enthusiasm that young people demonstrate when they are able to work with computers and get immediate responses of a correct answer or a mistake. If we agree that the student must learn what it is like to make decisions on his/her own and accept responsibility for his/her choices in life then we must provide such opportunities within the context of their school life. Children normally anticipate their first experiences of school life with openness and eagerness unless they have been frightened or intimidated by demands for perfection with harsh scolding or ridicule when they have made mistakes or unless they have been too tightly bound by overly dependent dynamics in the home. The young child normally has an inherent enthusiasm for learning and an openness to the experience. That is why young children pick up languages so easily compared to those of an older age. An inhibition to learning at an early age requires much more effort to extinguish later on and can be very costly to one's self-esteem. It is most important that primary school teachers not only be well versed in the pedagogy of their profession but also in the knowledge of child development. (See Appendix I.)

- *The Basic Needs of Children:* It is well recognized that the fundamental needs of children for adequate nourishment, safety, shelter, and social/emotional enrichment must be met if growth and learning toward productive and personally gratifying citizenship is to be expected. It has become clear that the dead-end and despairing government warehousing projects were the antithesis of healthy need fulfillment and produced an angry dependence of those hopelessly mired in the welfare system. This had to be corrected and, fortunately, is being corrected by legislation. We must encourage the development of communities that provide for all these basic needs much as we do for the elderly in retirement communities. They are a good model for what must be done to ensure healthy environments for children. It would be ideal if those two concepts (providing for the needs of children as well as the needs of older people) could be wedded because children benefit greatly from the influence of older people and older people benefit greatly from the presence and needs of children. Anyone who has seen this in operation in schools in which elderly people are brought into the school to assist the teacher as surrogate grandparents can testify as to how well this works. Healthy integrated communities can provide the attention children need as well as the day care for working mothers. A community support system can provide role model interactions that can open a young person's mind to the world at large with optimism and encouragement. It is damaging to child's basic need of belonging to be either held back or advanced to a higher-grade level in the earlier stages of development. They need to feel grounded in their social turf, so to speak.

Much of their social skills that they will carry with them in later life are established in those early school experiences. Considerations of advancement due to outstanding intellectual ability can be discussed with all concerned after those first four years, however, a better option would be to provide such a child encouragement and enrichment to engage in special projects and present them to the class. In such a classroom situation no child would be held back or prematurely advanced and all would get maximized learning experiences and attention to any deficits or disabilities because of a thorough pre-screening. No child would be held back during those first four years because it is an un-graded program. All children regardless of their learning aptitude would be brought up to speed with individualized instruction so by the time they are ready to enter a graded system they all have the basics skills required to succeed. Another consideration that ought to be addressed is the readiness of each particular child to enter the system in the first place. We have a rigid attitude that all children must be ready to start school formally at the age of five. This is an erroneous concept because children develop at differing rates. Some are ready at four and others not until they are six. Then why not have them start when they can demonstrate their readiness. They can be tested and screened not only for their readiness for formal schooling but also for any evidence of specific learning or developmental health problems. These can be effectively addressed when they can be most effectively remedied.

• *Counseling and Guidance:* The Problem of maintaining safety and orienting children to effective and productive living has become an increasingly vexing one in many schools particularly because children have become so frightened and hostile that many are resorting to using bullying and even weapons to resolve conflicts. Resolution of conflicts must be addressed at the time such situations occur and are the function of the school counselor but, unfortunately, counselors are often assigned to administrative duties while the administrator handles behavior problems. Counselors must be encouraged to practice their skills if they are to remain current and effective. We must understand that real security comes from within the person—not from more externalized rigid procedures and zero tolerance rules. Some innovative and creative endeavors have been undertaken in some school districts to curb destructive gang activity, bullying, and school avoidance by advancing a more inclusive environment. It can be asserted with some confidence that aggressive-hostile conflicts in the school are largely the result of unexpressed loneliness, isolation, and sadness—on the part of boys and girls. As a way of coping with these particular needs we could see the value of enlisting voluntary services of members of the working community. Individuals from various walks of life would come into the school for an hour a week to serve as models to emulate and learn from. It is frightening for a young person to be confronted with the prospect of having to find their way in the complex society of today without adults who are there and can show them the way with confidence. The value of counseling and guidance ought to be clear and highly prioritized. In addition to the function of enabling better social and emotional relations in the school, the counselor promotes an understanding of interests, abilities, talents, temperament, and values so they can relate themselves realistically and effectively to the "world of work" (see Appendix II) and intimate adult relationships (see Appendix III). This kind of self-discovery ought to begin in the primary grades and continue on up through the higher levels of education. The goal of education is to be a happy and productive citizen with a good stable mentality (see Appendix IV) who can make good choices and be responsible for those choices. This process ideally begins within the constellation of the family when parents are attentive enough toward their children that they can reflect important developmental information back to them and give them the right kind of care and attention they need. Children seldom get this kind of emotional support. Curricular programs ought to be geared more to the talents and abilities of the student so they can be encouraged and strengthened in their knowledge and understanding of themselves and the world-at-large. Not all students are academically inclined to deal with abstract and intuitive approaches to learning but are served in a better way if they can learn with a fuller use of their senses and motor capacities. That is why some progressive school systems offer alternative education and training can be customized for each individual student as to his/her propensities and interest patterns. While some are inclined toward working with their hands in a mechanical sense, others are inclined toward the arts, and others toward working with numbers. Others are more inclined toward the sciences, some in social services, while others are inclined towards fields of entrepreneurship. These personality types as they relate to the "world of work" are highly documented by career psychologists such as John Holland and are used as the gold standard for the study of individual career interests. Kids ought not to be strapped with conflicting educational experiences that dampen their enthusiasm. Not all are best served with a college education. Some are more adaptable to the trades and craftsmanship. This is not to say that young people ought to be allowed to skip the basic foundations and knowledge that provides the elements of their culture. We do not want cultural illiterates coming out of our schools who can decode words but can't understand the contextual meaning of what they read. What is advocated here is a curricula that takes into account more of the individual style of learning, more flexibility in scheduling and meshing of content material for the sake of greater relevance and meaning, more self-chosen projects, facilities for self-directed activities for both human and industrial skill development, and provisions for ongoing educational opportunities.

- *The Teacher as a Professional:* In order to restore education to its rightful place as a profession rather than the bureaucracy it has become, we must rethink the bifurcated caste system of the current educational administrative structure in America. It has become more like the military with an officer corps (administrators) on their own separate and higher salary schedule, on the one hand, and the enlisted corps (teachers) on the other. It could be argued that the teacher ought to be regarded as the true professional. The teacher's responsibility is far greater in the long run because he/she is impacting the minds and hearts and destiny of the student while the administrator provides the external structure. Unfortunately, the teacher has been relegated to a subordinate role in status and remuneration. The current school structure has become an authoritarian system with policy direction, curricular development and guidelines coming down the "chain of command" for the most part with very little input from those "on the line," so to speak, as to what the problems are and how they ought to be addressed. As a result the system has become demoralizing, stultifying and counter-productive. It thereby perpetuates ennui and resistance to change—change that is vitally needed especially in today's world. The growth of the administrator corps has spread to such an extent that many county jurisdictions, in many States, not only have their own school administrations with numerous specialized departments, as it is in the State of California, but, in addition, there are small individual school district administrations within each county representing superfluous and costly duplication of administrative functions. Also, with the reduction of funding in many schools you are likely to find a preferential priority for administrators and administrative salaries over that of teachers and counselors and this is an inappropriate allocation of funds.

- *The Relationship of Principal to Teacher and as Teacher:* At the end of Chapter 1 a brief mention was made of two retired school district superintendents: William Webster and John Stanford. Webster uses the term "principalship" to describe the role of principal as a teacher of teachers and he cites the following personal requirements of the learner-centered principal:

1. An informed vision of the school as an ideal setting for learner growth.
2. Skill and courage in exercising evaluative functions.
3. Confidence and ability to teach teachers for improved practices.
4. Ability to use the political dynamics of the school for learner benefit.
5. Sensitivity and finesse in all interpersonal relationships.
6. Aggressive instructional leadership that transcends "bandwagonism."
7. Integrity in leadership behavior.
8. Anticipatory, forward-thinking behavior.
9. An objective view of one's ideas and activities.
10. Strong convictions in the face of opposition.
11. A high level of stress tolerance.
12. The enabling skills of Continual Reasoned Adaptation (CRA).

In other words, principals must be totally involved in the process of educating the children of the district and continually adapting to those improvements needed to make sure every child achieves adequately and exits the system with viable skills and abilities. The principal must also be courageous enough to resist the pressures of conforming to the established "laissez faire" attitude which has so stultified progress and creativity. Too often the principal has concerned him or herself more with the structural and administrative functions, talking with parents and handling behavioral problems—the latter two being primarily the job of the counselors.

At the level of the teacher, Retired Major General John Stanford has described the need for a thorough and comprehensive system of standardized teaching methods and materials—much of which he learned from his 30 years of Army experience. To quote Stanford from his Army days teaching he says, "At the back of my classroom my book of lesson plans were open on a table outlining, exactly, what I was teaching that day, the week, that year. Each plan stated the learning objective for the lesson, along with the methods and material I'd use to teach. Each plan described the assessment tools I'd use to measure my students' learning and explained how the lesson supported the training objectives to follow. At defense training centers all across the country, similar lesson plans were open on the table, and they all taught the material the same way. The books wouldn't be identical: the Army gave us lots of leeway in developing our style and lessons. But our lesson plans were aligned horizontally from school to school and vertically from class to class to make sure that everybody who graduated as a helicopter and aircraft mechanic had mastered the same material."

- *The Modern High School:* Not all students are necessarily bound for higher academic education, but all well-educated adults ought to have had training in the practical aspects of living as they pass through the teenage years. Young people are noted for their energy, enthusiasm and much of that human resource is wasted and poorly directed. Sports are a good thing, but it won't carry over into adulthood as a useful skill. It is here suggested that half of the high school experience involve an apprenticeship program to supplement the academics during the Junior and Senior years. This would provide practical skills that suit the student's individual propensities such as crafts, banking and finances, real estate, business, the arts, drama, health and helping services, building, landscaping, agriculture, mechanics, civil safety, etc. If given the opportunity, teenagers are eager for meaningful responsibility to acquire useful skills and knowledge. For those who are not going on for higher education, this would fortify the young person with some real self-esteem based on acquired skills and knowledge in preparation for a productive life. Much of all this already exists in many high schools but only as an elective course and is not integrated into the community as an apprenticeship. It would also be suggested that slovenly dress not be allowed at school and only those who must get the jobs be allowed to drive cars to school. These new policies would apply to both girls and boys since the days of the docile and dependent female is a thing of the past.

CHAPTER SUMMARY

- The fact that society is becoming more complex places upon the educator a heavy responsibility for teaching to meet the challenges of the future and educating the young for competent and confident future citizenship.

- Education for the future will no longer be adequate for training only in specific skills and general knowledge, but must also include a greater understanding of self and other cultures and life style persuasions.

- At the primary/elementary levels of education, it is suggested that the grading system be updated to focus on developing confidence in one's own productions and efforts and acknowledging the individual's style of learning to support his/her interests and motivation.

- Along with providing for basic needs of each child is the necessity for effective counseling and guidance as to the individual's strengths and weaknesses, special interests and talents, temperament, and values so that the young person is better equipped to matriculate into meaningful employment and relationships in the future.

- The teacher must regain stature as a true professional with principals putting themselves more on the level of master teacher.

- The high school system must be re-structured in such a way as to provide practical life skills through apprenticeship programs in Junior and Senior years along with general education course work.

REVIEW QUESTIONS

- Describe how society becoming more complex.
- Why is it becoming necessary for students to gain more understanding of themselves and other cultures?
- How do you think grading system can be changed in order to enhance the student's confidence in his/her own work?
- Do you think acknowledging the individual's interests and motivations are helpful in learning? If so, why?
- Why do you think counseling and guidance would be helpful in choosing a career or occupation?
- Would you like to see more parity and teaching involvement between teachers and administrators? How could this help the overall function of educating the young?

CHAPTER 4

The American public school system must be made aware of its shortcomings and compelled to look to some of the modern innovative techniques for employee-management relations and employee inclusion models for establishing processes, goals, procedures, incentives, environmental aesthetics, and employee morale. Educators must regain their value as adult models for students as well as being competent in the educator role. Those early formative years in a child's school life are so important and those early grade teachers must be particularly well-trained and evaluated as to their effectiveness in getting student response, creating a friendly classroom atmosphere, establishing a feeling of security, exerting a stabilizing influence, inspiring originality and initiative, and developing student self-reliance. If teachers do not meet these standards, they must enter into training to achieve that degree of excellence. It is interesting to note that these standards for teacher evaluations have existed since 1938 when they were first published in the Journal of the National Education Association entitled, "Rating Teacher Personal Effectiveness." (See Appendix V.) This cannot be achieved when school staff personnel are demoralized by a bureaucratic and sub-professional system. What is required is a staff of highly effective teachers and support personnel who regard each other as respected colleagues in an important endeavor and who possess the qualities of integrity, open-mindedness, sincerity, objectivity, humility, courage, patience, discernment, competency and compassion and who can demonstrate to their students fairness, firmness, and friendliness. If one cannot demonstrate these high ideals of maturity and professional competence, then that individual ought not to be an educator. The school system ought not to be a haven or welfare port for the incompetent and uninspired. It ought to be a place for healthy, adequate personalities as models for young children.

Tenure at the elementary and high school level has become an insidious disease; a disease that has entered the blood stream of the system as a seduction for the weak and ineffective. This parasitical blight on the profession of education has somehow seeped down from the collegiate halls of academia and infiltrated the school system like an odorous fog. When good and conscientious teachers must work along with incompetent and uncaring individuals because they are protected by tenure and cannot be discharged, it is a continual source of frustration and aggravation to the dedicated teachers and a serious threat to students and their success as students. Tenure was originally established at the college level in order to insure a freedom of academic thought because students at the college level were thought to be adults and capable of using their own judgment and common sense about the thoughts and values espoused by a particular professor and his point of view. However, this is not appropriate for the lover grade levels where children's minds and character are yet to be guided and molded. The public school is the institution where parents can send their children to be taught not only the skills to become productive and gratified citizens but also to learn the most respected emotional/social character traits of the American culture and aspire to be the best they can.

Though there has been an insidious erosion of community trust and confidence in government and social processes in the past 40 or 50 years, those of the WWII era will often say that during the great world war this nation pulled together and worked together as a united community for the purpose of survival. That sense of communality and common purpose can and must be regained but without the condition of war. That is the great challenge of the future and we can succeed if we want to. Most humans, it is largely agreed, desire a living environment that values a sense of cooperation and goodwill rather than mistrust and alienation; a sense of community built on a common noble purpose rather than social estrangement and isolation. Maybe we have focused too much on the seductive powers of liberty and freedom and basic civil rights of individuals without attaching the true quality of those virtues to the concept of social responsibility. There may not be, in reality a true quality of liberty, freedom, justice or rights without a sense of social responsibility and connectedness. Whether it occurs on an individual basis or on societal basis and whether it occurs in the field of education, law, medicine, business, industry or politics, the society as a whole may be thwarted in its destined greatness unless all of us espouse the traditional values of social integrity that this country was founded upon. That is the crossing we all must make in order to feel reconnected to a noble national purpose and an ever-unfolding bright destiny. The way people rallied around those who were so devastated by the Oklahoma City bombing of 1995 and the wonderful acts of courage and compassion that came from all parts of this country ought to serve as an inspiration. It goes to show that the American people still possess that indefatigable character and social integrity that served us well in all the great crises of this Nation's history, in spite of all the indulgences of the past 50 years, we do live in a world of renewed hope. In the past 50 years we all lived with the terrible possibility of global nuclear destruction. The world has now seen the demise of the Communist Soviet Union and Russia is attempting to align with the Western world. There is international agreement that it is in everyone's best interests to contain and control the proliferation of nuclear weapons. Those dreaded missiles are no longer the global threat as before except perhaps for a small number of renegade countries who might wish to endorse terrorism for their own interests and even they can be dissuaded from evil intent. The United Nations is finding its role in the world and helping to maintain a fragile peace in the tangled ethnic divisions of the former Yugoslavia and the Middle East. Perhaps now if we can responsibly address our problems at home, we may begin to look optimistically to the future with confidence to build and create rather than destroy, to enter an era of mutually assured cooperation rather than "mutually assured destruction," and to educate and train rather than indulge in "projects" of despair.

There now appears to be an emerging consciousness of the implications of social/ethical values in the workplace and the need to recognize the importance of human considerations in modem living. Some of the great corporations in this country are discovering that it is in their best interests to provide consideration for such human needs as flex time, in-house child care, maternity and/or paternity leave, counseling for those who must be reassigned or have need for resolving personal crises, work-out facilities and healthy lunch counters, coordinating with high schools in the process of matriculating young people into the labor market and assuring that they are suitably trained and directed, and a generally more socially synergistic work environment. It is becoming more apparent that a need-gratified employee is a more productive employee who can cope more effectively with the demands of the ever increasing technologies.

The people's righteous anger is rising against the forces of impotence and negativity and, as had been the case in the past, when the American people are provoked to justifiable anger and greater awareness the Ship of State will be reset on its true course while new technological systems and viable cultural values will assume a direction of purpose and thoughtful intention. There does appear to be changes in the wind. There is a new and exciting concept in education that does not yet have a full consensus of the American people but it is growing in strength in various areas of the United States. It is characterized by an integration of the community and the school in a more dynamic and synergistic way. It stresses a melding of school and various community resources. It brings into focus the needs of educating children from a wider perspective, i.e. from the point of view of involved parents, educators, community policing and law, medical and mental health workers, and those in business and industry. Schools under the new system would be kept open as channels for learning and community problem solving, such as libraries are kept open (or ought to be) to the public as resource facilities and used for children's after school activities. Older, retired people would be brought into the schools as surrogate grandparents to offer emotional as well as educational support.

Promoting a revival of the American hope for the future and the revitalization of the society is by a whole-hearted support of two of society's most important institutions, the family and the public schools. In the final analysis, it is not a question of whether or not the public school system can be saved. It must be saved, otherwise the society will be dominated by an educational elite. The public school system is the only institution that assures a broadly based educated populace as this democratic republic requires so that it may maintain and enhance itself in perpetuity. I say let the focus for renewal first be placed upon the schools and the neighborhoods of those schools because that is where the hopes and dreams of parents, through their children, can begin to move in an upward direction. The public schools are where the minds, bodies, and spirits of the children of America can be molded with strengths and the faith needed for the future. It is also the place in which real opportunity and independence can be fostered through the acquisition of life and workplace skills and self-understanding. Let us think, therefore, of hope for the future through opportunity in the public school system as the key concept of American education. We only need give it a new vitality and enthusiasm. I believe the United States has a unique destiny to become the beacon of light to the world, but we are letting that precious beacon grow dim. Let us stand on the side of light rather than darkness.

CHAPTER SUMMARY

- An old axiom among psychologists is that you can't start solving a problem until you first acknowledge it. With reference to the school systems in America, it does appear that there is a resistance to acknowledging shortcomings and making changes that will adapt to the challenges of the 21st century. In the past children were regimented into a lock-step rote learning mode that was suitable for employment in a manufacturing economy. A worker could offer his skills with loyalty to a company and be well assured of a job throughout his working life with a gold watch and reliable pension upon retirement. That type of employment is becoming rarer and the schools must be reconfigured to meet the skill demands of the 21st century labor market. The world is becoming more interactive and complex every day. In order for a democratic republic to prevail, the populace must be educated to understand the real issues confronting the society.

- Since education is also a matter of building character in the young, it is important that teachers and educators meet higher professional standards of effectiveness. That would include such qualities as creating a friendly classroom atmosphere, establishing a feeling of security, exerting a stabilizing influence, inspiring originality and initiative, and developing student self-reliance.

- Tenure at the primary/elementary and secondary levels ought to be reconsidered for the sake of keeping an edge on the effectiveness of teachers and insuring that those who are not in keeping with standards of excellence should be let go and guided toward other occupations more suitable to their interests and skills.

- The public school systems must rededicate themselves to the noble purpose of enhancing communal attitudes of goodwill and connectedness and building confidence and trust in the American way of life. Community leaders must promote social-ethical values in the workplace, such as flex-time, in-house child care, maternity and paternity leave, counseling for those that must be reassigned or have need for resolving personal crises, work-out facilities, and healthy lunch counters—and coordinating with the high schools in the process of matriculating young people into the labor market so they can be assured of suitable training and direction in the interests of a more synergistic work environment.

• Children must be educated from a wider perspective taking into account the whole range of community activities. Schools ought to be kept open, much as libraries are (or should be), to serve as resources for community problem solving and after school activities. The public schools are the only institutional establishment that can insure an educated populace for the perpetuity of a democratic-republic society and serve as an opportunity for each individual to cultivate their best aspirations and dreams.

REVIEW QUESTIONS

• Why is it important to reconfigure the public school systems for the 21st century?
• Why is it important that teachers be held to higher standards of character and competence?
• Is tenure at the primary/elementary and secondary levels a good thing or a bad thing and why?

- Can you give reasons why a broader perspective of education by involving the community at large can facilitate better educational outcomes?
- Do you think that serving the personal needs of employees can improve efficiency and effectiveness on the job?
- How can keeping the schools open later (much as libraries are) improve the welfare of children?

APPENDIX I

(Please note; All subsequent pages must be exactly as they appear in text)

UNPUBLISHED NOTES FROM LECTURES ON CHILD DEVELOPMENT

by Richard C. Kogl, M.D.
1979, Belmont, California

THE INFANT (BASIC TRUST VS MISTRUST)

The psychosocial strength characterized by successful achievement of this developmental task is HOPE and FAITH.

The developmental task of infancy is the establishment of Basic Trust. According to Erik Erikson, Basic Trust is promoted between the child and parent when there is time for relaxed and enjoyable attention. All children crave and need this kind of attention every day between birth and approximately 18 months. Game playing, such as peek-a-boo and hide-and-seek, reassure the child that there can be brief separations from the parent without becoming a major crisis. This kind of activity enables the child to risk further separations and thereby build self-confidence and a sense of autonomy. A child cannot be spoiled at this stage of development. By being totally attentive to the child's physical and emotional needs he/she comes to see that the world and the important people in it are basically friendly and loving.

Infants who are denied this kind of nurturance to a severe degree very often fail to develop a capacity to relate to others and become deeply alienated and resentful. They characteristically either turn their resentment inward toward themselves or outward toward society in general. Many of our socially and psychologically disordered adults can trace the origin of their problems to a lack of Basic Trust in the early formative years of life. Since each stage of development is built upon the one preceding it, a correction or remediation must take place early or the pathology will persist and become reinforced.

The infant, having developed the trust to feel attached or bonded to the significant caregiver, can now achieve the ability to gradually separate from the parent through the inner confidence that the most important human being will return soon enough. This is why peek-a-boo games are important learning tasks for an infant at this stage of development; it is training for the experience of un-anxious separations and out of these experiences of separation also come the ability to sustain loss and cope with grief. One of the most valuable gains from acquiring Basic Trust is the ability to experience and deal with loss as part of living.

The problematic consequences to not learning how to deal with loss or how to grieve effectively, are the following:

1. Feelings of emptiness that can give rise to behavioral acting-out, such as stealing, a need to constantly feed oneself with food, sex, drugs or other addictive compulsions.
2. Unrequited grief can also leave a child or adolescent vulnerable, which can result in behavior such as denial or hiding from the realities of life. Feelings of such helplessness or passivity can leave one a target for victimization or exploitation and thereby set the stage for

negative attitudes of unworthiness, anger, and depression, to name a few.

By 3 months:

- Smiles spontaneously and then responsively
- Grasps rattle, reaches for objects but misses them
- Laughs or squeals; vocalizes without crying
- While on stomach, lifts head 45 to 90 degrees and able to hold head steady and erect
- Rolls over from stomach to back

By 4 to 6 months:

- Nonspecific reflexes fade, replaces with more specific behavior such as reaching and babbling
- Can resist toy pull
- Can grasp toy
- Can turn toward voices
- Can sustain some weight bearing on legs; there is no lagging of head when pulled to a sitting position and can sit with support
- Weight doubles by 6 months; weight gain of 5 to 7 oz. per week in first 6 months
- Teething generally begins around 6 months; first two teeth are central lower incisors.
- By 7 to 9 months:
- Initially shy with strangers, usually occurs at 6 to 8 months and is normal; indicates attachment between infant and care-giver

- Child will usually repeat over and over newly learned behaviors, such as sitting or standing
- Weight gain of 3 to 5 oz. per week in second 6 months
- Can feed self crackers
- Play peek-a-boo games
- Struggles for toy out of reach
- Can take two cubes in hands and bang them together
- Can pass cube hand-to-hand
- Babbles; says "mama"/"dada" but is non-specific
- Gets self up to sitting position
- Pulls self standing position
- Stands holding on

By 10 to 12 months:

- Plays pat-a-cake and plays ball
- Indicates wants without crying
- Drinks from a cup
- Is able to grasp with fingers
- "Dada"/"Mama" is now specific
- Stands alone well
- Walks holding on
- Stoops and recovers
- Height increases by about 50% by first birthday
- By the end of first year 6 to 8 teeth have emerged

By 12 to 18 months:

- Imitates housework
- Uses spoon, spilling little
- Removes own clothes
- Scribbles spontaneously
- Build tower with cubes
- Has three word vocabulary other than "mama/"dada"
- Points to at least one named body part
- Kicks a ball
- Walks up steps one at a time
- Has a wide-based gait, i.e. walks like a duck

THE TODDLER (Autonomy vs. Self-Doubt)

The psychosocial strength characterized by successful achievement of this developmental task is WILL and INTENTIONALITY.

At this stage of development, according to Erik Erickson, there is muscular maturation in which the major theme is to hold on to or let go in speech, weaning from the bottle, physical mobility, toileting, sleeping and expressions of feelings—especially anger. The question is, "how much power do I have over parts of my body as opposed to how much power do others have over parts of me" and "how vulnerable are the parts of my body?"

The parent or "significant other" at this time takes on the role of limit setter, naysayer and punisher and the younger the child, the quicker he/she wants mother-the-punisher to transform back to mother-the-comforter. The more trust the child has in the "return" of mother-the-comforter, the more he/she feels free to "flex" his/her autonomy muscles. The trust now refers not to a physical return, but rather to the return of a "you are ok validation." Sufficient trust allows us to keep our security and our power issues relatively separate. If security and power issues are too tightly intertwined it produces adults (later on) who give double messages such as "say no to me to prove you care for me." Chronic inhibition of power serves to retain the feeling of placating the comforting and forgiving parents and promotes a wish to be forever passive.

As changes in the "self" and "self-image" emerge, the child senses that he/she is being judged by others. Soon the child begins to judge himself or herself. This self-appraisal is the source of the self-image. When the family and parents are not trustworthy and supportive collaborators in the autonomy task, maladaptive or behaviors and a negative self-image develops resulting in roles that support such games as passive/dependency, passive/aggressive, hostile/aggressive, or schizoid/withdrawal and incompetency manifestations.

Mental acts in fantasy are dry runs for action in the real world. How quickly one shifts from fantasy to the real world depends upon the feedback from the world. When massive amounts of doubt develop then acts in the fantasy world proliferate while acts in the real world are cautious, tentative, poorly planned and consist of stereotypes and repetitive games and roles. A healthy self-image results in, "I feel powerful enough in this world to be able to negotiate in good faith with others, to work out power balances, to compromise, to sacrifice some of what I wish without going to the extreme of being a doormat and to insist upon some of what I wish without going to the extreme of being a bully, tyrant or prima donna. I can feel free to experiment with a variety of behaviors and a variety of roles without being crippled by shame or doubt. I cannot be fully self-indulgent and I must begin to have sensitivity to the needs and wishes of others. I can live together with people in this world.

By 19 to 24 months:

- Puts on clothing
- Washes and dries hands
- Helps with simple tasks
- Build tower with 4 cubes
- Imitates vertical line
- Combines words
- Names one picture
- Follows two or three directions
- Throws ball overhand
- Jumps in place

By 24 to 36 months:

- Dresses with supervision
- Plays interactive games such as tag
- Copies a circle
- Builds tower with 8 cubes
- Uses plurals
- Gives first and last name
- Balances on one foot briefly

THE PRE-SCHOOLER
(Initiative vs Guilt)

The psychosocial strength characterized by successful achievement of this developmental task is PURPOSE and DIRECTIONALITY.

Roughly between the ages of three and five, there are major issues to be mastered around the developmental stage which Erikson calls "initiative." Two issues are gender identity and guilt. After one has passed through the earlier stage of autonomy (or recognition that one can intend to do something and can indeed do something (i.e. one can act and cause an effect), the child is interested in challenging his or her own body to express itself in ways of play, manipulating tools or toys and in the emerging sexuality. This means an enthusiastic emersion into the world and treating it as if it belonged to the child. It is at this time that gender identity is being established wherein a young boy identifies with his father and comes to love the mother from a distance, so to speak. The girl, on the other hand, achieves her own distance from the mother by acquiring the mother's role and identifying with her. The term "distance" here is used to mean a sense of separateness or boundary that establishes the self of the child from the parent; thereby, moving away from the symbiotic tie to the mother to an internalized portable parent. The child becomes more independent of the mother as a result of normal independence, the child may introject, by induction, the mother's fear and develop a "school phobia."

Both the child and parent must know that the separation process is a normal movement toward the personal autonomy started in the earlier stage of development. Another important task which success in being included in the triad (the parent's relationship) or too much "success" (feeling favored over the other parent) may make sharing of the relationship problematic. The best balance is for the child to feel importantly included in the family but not intimately included in the marriage dyad, as in such situations where a girl becomes the object of the father's needs or the boy becomes he must come to identify himself as distinctly different from his mother and that is why it is important that there be a significant adult male in the boy's life to support him through this transition. The quality of this transition process may be gentle or harsh depending on whether the culture wants to force boys to become tough and fearless warriors and girls to become clinging, dependent and passive servants or something more egalitarian.

Sexual interests and concerns emerge at this stage. Anatomical curiosity concerns both sexes and a major risk at this time is for either gender to see themselves or the other as "bad." A child benefits from contact and support from adults and children of both sexes. There is also collecting and internalization of opposite sex traits, attitudes and feelings around female sensitivities for boys and male sensitivities for girls. If too much of these sensitivities are buried or repressed for boys and male sensitivities for girls. If too much of these sensitivities are buried or repressed out of fear, the person is diminished as a total human being. Although a highly stereotyped hyper-masculine boy or an ultra-feminine girl may find childhood simpler because of the one dimensional nature of their roles, adolescence and adulthood may be stressful because then more complex identities are required.

Also, simultaneously, the child must become capable of feeling guilt. Guilt reduction is as important as guilt production and is related to the capacity for empathy which is a marker for true socialization. The child must learn that guilt can be reduced through the hope of genuine reparation, remorse, and reconciliation. It must be produced to stimulate responsibility for wrong-doing or injury of another human being or to oneself. Guilt is not to be confused with shame, which is deeper feeling of wounding to the core of one's personality. To feel shame is to feel that one is a flawed person with questionable capacity for redemption. Since we are flawed in some way we must also learn that one can be flawed and still be valued, worthwhile, and acceptable. A parent can do great harm to a child by inflicting shame often as way of manipulating or controlling and constantly making reference to the "flaw" in the child's character or personhood. Guilt can also be a destructive way of manipulating a child's behavior by not allowing for the kind of reparation and healing that can be forgiving. If a child is made to feel that there is no hope of making things right again, then it becomes a corrosive catalyst in the personality of the individual. Guilt can be thought of as a kind of empathy that comes as a result of an aggressive activity that produces harm to someone. When a child is using his new found power, initiative, and intentionality to get what he or she wants or desires and someone gets hurt in the process, then one must learn to feel guilt or empathy of the other in order to become socialized and in this way take steps to correct or at least ameliorate the behavior. An absence, therefore, of socialized guilt either does not provide the necessary restraints or there is too much of a feeling of disenfranchisement and unworthiness to initiate oneself into the world.

The masteries, therefore, required for a child by the age of five in order to move up the ladder of development are the following:

1. A sense of bodily intactness as in "My body belongs to me."
2. A sense of gender role and identity.
3. A sense of stability in the family and the parent's relationship.
4. A sense of safety and permission to explore the world and be curious.
5. A feeling of security of his/her place in the family including the feeling that he/she has neither too little nor too big a part in the marital relationship.
6. A sense that one can live and flourish in a triadic relationship.
7. An inner sense of what is right and wrong.

<u>DEVELOPMENTAL MILESTONES (Ages 3 to 5)</u>

- Attempts to perform activities of daily living independently
- Attempts to make things for self and others
- Tries to "help"
- Talks constantly; verbally explores the world; asks "why?"
- Extremely active; highly creative imagination and indulges in fantasy and magical thinking
- May demonstrate fear of "monsters" and dark rooms
- Able to tolerate short periods of separation
- Child needs encouragement to dress self by providing simple clothing
- Can be assigned small simple tasks or errands
- Questions must be answered patiently and simply. Do not offer child more information than he/she asking for
- Child needs to reminded to go to the bathroom. Tends to forget
- It is normal to have "imaginary playmates" at this stage
- Offer realistic support and reassurance with regard to fears
- Expose to a variety of experiences such as the zoo, train rides and shopping
- Enroll in preschool or nursery school program and prepare for kindergarten at five but age at starting kindergarten should have some flexibility due to variation of developmental

and maturational differences. Entrance to kindergarten ought to be permissible between four and six depending on the readiness of the child

- Child continues slow and steady growth; generally more in height than weight and appears taller and thinner and "pot belly" of toddler gradually disappears
- All 20 "baby" teeth are present and child ought to have annual dental check-ups and daily brushing to be a matter of routine
- Visual acuity ought to be 20/30 between ages three and five and hearing and vision screening ought to be performed before kindergarten

Specifically by age 3 years:

- Can button clothing
- Can separate from mother easily
- Can pick longer of two lines
- Beginning to use scissors
- Comprehends "cold," "tired," and "hungry"
- Comprehends prepositions such as "over" and "under"
- Recognizes colors
- Pedal tricycle
- Broad jumps and jumps in place
- Balances on one foot

Specifically by age 4 years:

- Brushes own teeth and combs own hair
- Dresses without supervision

- Knows own age and birthday
- Eats with a fork
- Ties own shoes
- Draws person with three body parts
- Better use of scissors
- Knows two or three opposite analogies, i.e. dog can bark, a cat can't bark
- Defines 6 to 9 words
- Can follow 2 or 3 simple directions
- Can hop on one foot
- Can catch a bounced ball
- Can walk heel-to-toe

Specifically by age 5 years:

- Shows interest in money
- Knows days of the week and seasons
- Can print own name
- Can draw person with six body parts
- Can count to ten
- Can verbalize number sequences such as phone numbers
- Attempts to ride a bike
- Attempts to roller-skate, jump rope, and bounces ball with some success
- Can walk backward heel-to-toe

SCHOOL AGE AND PRE-ADOLESCENT

(Industry vs Inferiority—ages 6 through 12)

The psychosocial strength characterized by successful achievement of this developmental task is COMPETENCE and ASCENDENCY.

Erik Erikson describes this stage as having the developmental task of achieving "industry" over "inferiority." The importance and crucial issue at this age level is the achievement of a sense of competence. Human cultures have taken advantage of the child's new capabilities in this age group and begin a more intensive indoctrination of the child. Simultaneously, the child hungers to master skills which will more closely identify him/her with his/her culture. Throughout most of human history, survival tasks were learned at the side of the same sex parent and other older family members. The child rarely held any doubts about the relevance of what he or she was doing or learning.

Erikson has turned the task at this age "industry" or the quest for mastery and competence. In the pre-industrial era, the child imitated his/her elders (those elders with whom he/she had the closest emotional ties) in learning techniques which had highly apparent and tangible value such as farming or weaving. In the industrial society complicated and costly machines and complex and expensive managerial systems had to be learned largely away from those with whom one had close emotional ties. A child had to learn the fundamental units of education for becoming an industrial producer, i.e. reading, writing, and arithmetic. The acquisition of these skills which were less immediately relevant to the child were taught by a designated specialist or teacher. As the post-industrial society emerged, values changed in that the work ethic as the ultimate definition of the meaning of life receded in importance. Then there emerged a growing concern as to just what were the relevant skills to reach a child for survival in a post-industrial society—particularly since the rate of change had been accelerating. What seems to be emerging in modern times is the need to know one's personal assets, abilities and skills and also how to access information through high technology in order to implement those assets, abilities and skills.

Other characteristics of this age group is more movement toward autonomy and yet more awareness of the importance of peer relations and acknowledgement of authority figures. The school becomes the first significant institution which differentiates children on the basis of achievement and behavior. After the age of six, the child increasingly considers his/her peers' judgment to have power. He/she seeks approval from both adults and peers and recognizes discrepancies in how he/she is judged by the two groups. There is a new need for belonging, i.e. a wish to belong to a group or a circle of playmates and the counterpart aversion to being an outsider. Unlike the family boundaries, peer group boundaries are highly fluid and this must be more carefully guarded. The child needs to learn how to be a member of an in-group while learning not to de-humanize outsiders.

The child has the power to become a conformist to his/her peer group and usually exercises this power. Trustworthiness in the sense of reliability and responsibility develops. Reliability and responsibility are important at home and in the school but are even more powerfully reinforced by the peer group. This is where the child learns who he/she is as a person independent of adult judgments and evaluations. Rules and fair play become more sophisticated and more valued at this stage.

Typically, boy's groups are highly "counter-phobic" and much pressure is put on boys not to be afraid of things. Competitiveness and aggressiveness become important values but the intensity and degree depends upon the needs of the society and their own traditional attitudes. To what degree these values are learned traits of biologically based is still unclear; however, it seems both factors are involved. This is an interesting study for those who wish to take up the anthropological implications.

The reassuring "home base" now becomes more complicated since it takes on a triple aspect, i.e. the family, the internalized parent, and the peer group. Problems which may arise at this age are in the form of unyielding parents who undermine the emotional shift toward peers. The self is now taking on the aspect of a Persona (a public person), a Shadow (a hidden and perhaps non-conforming or rebellious aspect) and the Anima (female sensitivity) or Animus (male sensitivity). All these dimensions of the emerging and growing personality serve to enrich the individual but can also cause internal conflicts and disturbances if not assimilated.

The issue of cruelty emerges. Treating human beings as an object is a dangerous narcotic. Children will turn to this narcotic if they are not helped to learn other ways to deal with each other as in the "Lord of the files." The other side of this cruelty aspect is the child who is so afraid of being cruel or being treated cruelly that he/she goes to the extreme of seeking a frictionless world.

Death also becomes a reality during this stage of development. The reality and acceptance of the eventual death of all living things including such important persons as one's own parents reflects greater maturity and so grief-work mechanisms can be more accessible. As was mentioned earlier in the infancy stage of development, grief is handled more effectively when Basic Trust was established beforehand and separations were learned to be more tolerated realistically.

Important educational goals that merit consideration for this school age group are self-esteem, responsibility and will or intentionality/ educational goals in the pre-industrial era were the acquisition of practical survival skills in which authority was found. Educational goals in the industrial society were the acquisition of skills and values (or choices) and authority was found in the written word along with the advent of the public school system.

In the post-industrial society, values, skills and the written word required a buttressing of intentionality or the obverse would be a degeneration into a "schizoid" powerlessness and passivity through lack of will and emotion.

This age of six through 12 is generally thought of as pre-adolescence and as much is characterized by much overlap of developmental tasks and marked individual differences. Chronological age of puberty varies and chronological age is not perfectly correlated with developmental age. There is a steady drop throughout this century of the average age at which puberty occurs. Harry Stack Sullivan describes this period as the time when "chums" and altruism become important along with "consensual validation" because there is a greater degree of intimacy in the special friend relationship. This relationship offers a chance to check out with someone else one's view of oneself and the world. This has a socializing and a freeing effect because it is the start of objectivity and compassion or the "stepping out of one's own skin." Failure at this step can result in the person tending to remain self-centered, grandiose and afraid of the world. Fortunately, an upsurge in libido in adolescence produces an upsurge in social interests. It is the more fortunate adolescent who has already created the foundation of social interest in preadolescence. Along with the curiosity and fascination with the body and sexual capacities, pre-adolescence is a time for manifesting great emphasis and exaggeration such as idealism about the world and altruistic friendships. Hero worship is common at this age. There is also a great concern about bodily power and humankind and these become inter-related as destructive fantasies and activities with the notion that "there is power in my body to destroy or create." With this we can see the emergence of gang activity, which can become destructive, such as the "bloods" and the "crips" or other gang-like activity such as the Boy Scouts of America, which is creative and productive.

The pre-adolescent is also struggling with a number of ambiguities such as:

1. The body as a source of pride or shame, wonder or disgust, weakness or power, masculinity or femininity, repulsiveness or attractiveness.
2. Questions such as, "I am significant or important in the world at large and what will I do in the world?"
3. Questions such as, "am I good or bad?"

At this pre-adolescent stage of development the ability to conceptualize abstractly gives the world a new reality and provides the ability to form rich symbols and symbolic fantasies. The symbolic fantasies about his/her in the large world give him/her new mental leverage for living in the small worlds of the family, school, neighborhood, and community.

SCHOOL AGE DEVELOPMENT MILESTONES

- Moving toward complete independence
- May be very competitive and wants to achieve in school and at play
- Likes to be alone occasionally and may seem shy
- Child wants to be accepted as he/she is
- Needs consistent support and guidance
- Has difficulty handling excessive authority or excessive demands
- Almost doubles in weight from six to 12
- Period of slow and steady growth
- One to two inches per year in height
- Three to six pounds per year in weight
- Begins to lose primary teeth
- Eruption of permanent teeth, including molars, and has 26 permanent teeth by age 12
- Dental screening annually and daily brushing
- Vision should be screened annually. Usually at school
- Vision well established at 20/20 between 9 and 11 years
- Pubescence onset for girls at 10 and boys at 12
- The start of a growth spurt
- Some sexual changes may start to occur of primary and secondary sex characteristics

Specifically by six to eight years:

- Child is dramatic, exuberant and with boundless energy
- Child has alternating periods of quiet and private behavior
- Child is conscientious and punctual
- Wants to care for own needs but also needs reminders and supervision
- Is oriented to time and space
- Learns to read, tell time and follow a map
- Is interested in money and asks for an "allowance"
- Eagerly anticipates upcoming events, trips, etc.
- Can ride a bike, swim, play ball

Specifically by nine to twelve years:

- Child worries over tasks and takes things seriously, yet also developing a sense of humor and likes to tell jokes
- Keeps room, clothes and toys relatively tidy
- Enjoys physical activity and has great stamina
- Is very enthusiastic at work and play and has lots of energy and may fidget, drum fingers or tap foot
- Want to "work" to earn money by mowing lawns, baby-sitting or delivering papers
- Loves secrets and being in secret clubs
- Is very well behaved outside his/her own home or with company

- Can use tools/equipment and follow directions or recipes
- By twelfth birthday a paradoxical stormy behavior sets in as the onset of

ADOLESCENCE

(Identity Formation vs Identity or Role Confusion)

The psychosocial strength characterized by successful achievement of this developmental task is FIDELITY and LOYALTY.

This is the developmental stage in which identity competes with role confusion and the following markers define the transition from childhood to adolescence in preparation for adulthood. There are changes in body image related to sexual development. An awkwardness and lack of coordination is followed by development in major musculature during early adolescence. Gradually, the awkwardness smooths out as time goes on. There is much interest in the opposite sex with females learning toward the "romantic" and males toward the "adventurous." Many want to be exactly like their peers and can even become hostile toward parents, adults, and family. There is growing concern with vacation and life after high school. Parents can offer firm but realistic limits on behavior and continue to offer guidance and support which may or may not be heeded limits on behavior and continue to offer guidance and support which may or may not be heeded at any given time, however, the parental input is important nevertheless. Adolescents are now allowed to earn their own money and control their own finances. It is important to assist the adolescent in the development of a positive self-image during this period of growth along with much acknowledgement of his/her special abilities and attributes.

According to Erikson the major life task for the adolescent is the establishment of identity and there are three aspects to this like task at this stage and they are:

1. Attachment to persons
2. Management of Daemonic forces (passions)
3. Role in society vs role confusion

When considering the various dimensions of family structures, we can see an evolutionary process beginning with the traditional extended family which provided a fairly simple transition from childhood to adulthood. From the traditional there was a movement toward the nuclear family of the industrial society in which each was brand new unit with a brand new life. The sense of individuality was much greater with nuclear families. With the individualism of nuclear families came a sense of disconnectedness and lack of family continuity which added more stress to adolescent separation issues. The peer group became an even stronger influence in the life of the adolescent. The rapid move away from the family in early adolescence could produce considerable feelings of isolation and in many ways the peer group became the substitute of the family as it has in gang activity. One variation of this need for connectedness was a shift to adults rather than peers which led to association with cult figures. Still another variation on this theme was to try and skip adolescence altogether and move directly into a pseudo-adult intimate relationship with the usual sever adjustment problems later on.

Secondly, the successful assimilation of the Daemonic forces in adolescent development should not be overlooked because that is what provides the powerful leverage or motivation for true emancipation and matriculation into the adult world. Three examples of the Daemonic forces which fundamentally tie into the primitive "smell" brain and basic "signal" behavior are the following:

1. Tenderness and compassion and the wish to nurture, which is a wish for physical contact, protecting, and caring for the young of the species and also crying—the signal which evokes a primitive response to apply tenderness.
2. Rage and anger in which one must make a distinction between true rage and anger.
3. Direct assault or invasion of one's psychological boundaries or territory and anger—a communication of a feeling of threat that one must not step further into one's psychological or physical territory.
4. Lust as a Daemonic force needs to be truly assimilated if adjustment to adulthood is to be firmly established. Erotic feelings are felt by children, but not with the same intensity as after puberty and there are two kinds of adolescent problems regarding lust, i.e. the first is that any tenderness or affection is sometimes confused with or is thought to be the same as lust and

the second problem that may arise is that lust is thought to equal rape or sexual exploitation. The adolescent they can come together as in a good marriage and when they do come together, they strongly enhance the relationship. Also the adolescent must fully accept and acknowledge his/her own lustful feelings, but only when those feelings are acted out irresponsibly and without empathy for the other person can it be thought of as sexual exploitation or rape. The thrust and power of the Daemonic forces in late adolescence, while earlier used primarily as leverage for emancipation, now becomes paramount in their own need for expression and the vehicle for expression is through the newly developing individual identity. Expression is effected through imitation and role playing, as well through introspection, self-searching, reflection, and discussion. Techniques of expression without purpose produces robots or puppets while purposes without technique produces paralysis. One must not only have skills, but direction and motivation as a ship must have power, direction and the capacity to stay afloat.

Finally, the adolescent is much more concerned about the relevance of what he/she is learning. During pre-adolescence, special friendships and consensual validation are very important as are heroes and heroines and these tend to be used increasingly for "how to do it" exercises. In adolescence there is less value in escapist fantasies and much more value in finding ways to enter the real world of adulthood. The adolescent begins to search for an adult identity which will suffice for him/her and the requirements of the world. In late adolescence, the intimacy issue tends to be similar to the requirements of the world. In late adolescence, the intimacy issue tends to be similar to the intimacy concerns of adults; however, identity tends to remain predominate. Generative concerns of adolescence (a later developmental task of adulthood) tend to be pseudo-generative. The philosophical interests and concerns of adolescence superficially resemble the interests which form the ego-integrity task of later years but it is more of a "head trip" for the adolescent and more of a "gut issue" for the older person. Sometimes over-repressed or over-restrained adolescents will side step more immediate issues and rather channel their energy into philosophical-generative concerns and intellectually grapple with attempting to "solve the problems of the world."

Acquiring an adult identity has many components, two of which are emancipation and individuality and, in this regard, the important questions asked by the adolescent are:

1. "Who am I?"
2. "If I regress can I be assured that I will not be locked in or held on to, i.e. my growth depends on mobility?"
3. "If I strive for autonomy, independence and power, will this produce problems of doubt,

shame, contingent validation or selective validation?"

The early part of adolescence is characterized by rapid and dramatic physical and physiological changes. The sum of these changes cause a shattering challenge to the child's identity and the adolescent begins to ask, "Who Am I?" The "Who Am I" question as it emerges is the start of the adolescent identity task which is primarily a socio-cultural phenomenon triggered by chrono-biological issues. That simply means that when a young boy or girl enters puberty, the society and therefore the young person must try to figure out just how he can become this contributing member. In the pre-industrial cultures, the adult-child differentiation tented to be so simple that it often could be dealt with by an initiation rite. Being an adult in an industrial culture was more complex and ambiguous and generally entailed a break a break with the family of origin. The economic motive in the industrial society promoted individualism on a mass scale with a consequent increase in "freedom" and decrease in "security." One had the freedom of leaving the constraints of the small farming community and seeking factory work in the big city but the consequent feeling of up-rootedness and isolation led to a sense of loss of inner security that one enjoyed in the home town community. Individualism and the emancipation from the family made adolescence a new problem for the human race.

Something ought to be said about parenting the adolescent. There are three kinds of intrusive parenting:

1. Total control more appropriate for the younger child.
2. Selective over-control with poor judgment as to the areas of over-control.
3. Over-control coupled with role reversal and manipulation.

As was mentioned before, adolescence is a time of gradual emancipation along with movement toward greater autonomy and individuality and a struggle for adult identity. Over-control is antagonistic to this process. Thoughtful and compassionate negotiation is a better approach to take. Values of mutual respect, trust, loyalty and integrity are needed with one's adolescent children even in spite of the often adolescent oppositional, rebellious and even hostile behavior. We sometimes forget in our society that it is the parent that is supposed to be the "gold standard" of behavior and not the adolescent. In a discussion of American style parenting of the adolescent it ought also to be mentioned that with some there is a tendency to over-protect and/or indulge the child until he/she is 18 years of age and then expect them to suddenly take on the responsibilities of adulthood with the added burden of guilt for not appreciating all the parents have done for them over the years. The process of emancipation, individuation and identity ought to be thought of as a process of gradualism, support, understanding, and growing responsibility.

There is often confusion of values that makes it more difficult to answer the "what is an adult" question. Although the peers are a source of surface identity supplies, core identity comes from the definition of and by adults.

Often adults lacking in core identity themselves are phobic of adolescents because young people seek out the core and the young people are distasteful of the "phoniness" which often accompanies lack of core identity. Often the "core-less" adults attempt to co-opt the youth identity in their own hunger for identity. This makes it difficult for the young person to establish a sense of separateness and emancipation. Where no core identity is presented and where parents co-opt the transitional youth identity there is a surface continuity which paradoxically prevents a true coming together of the generations. True coming together is based on mutuality that includes a recognition and a respect for differences.

In conclusion, late adolescence ends when a successful resolution and a balance is struck between the Daemonic and the identity where identity is resilient enough to survive being "lost" to passion. The Daemonic must be channeled and expressed through the person's own identity and the last marker for the end of adolescence is by some kind of identity commitment such as a career choice. It ought to be noted that as our society has become more complex the period of adolescence has extended well into the 20s because of the difficulty of making a commitment to a career choice and career choice necessarily precedes a commitment to start a family.

ADOLESCENT DEVELOPMENTAL MILESTONES

- Adolescent growth spurt lasts 24 to 36 months
- Growth in height commonly ceases at 16 to 17 years in girls and 18 to 20 in boys
- Boys gain more weight than girls and are generally taller and heavier
- By 18 to 21 years 32 permanent teeth are present

For Females:

- Increase in transverse diameter of pelvis
- Enlargement of breasts
- Change in vaginal secretions
- Growth of pubic hair
- Menstruation commences on a average at 12 years but can range from nine to 18 years.

For Males:

- Enlargement of genitals
- Swelling of chest
- Growth of pubic, axillary, facial and body hair
- Lowering of voice
- Production of sperm on average at 14 years

Motor Development:

- Early: awkward, uncoordinated, poor posture, decrease in energy and stamina

- Later: increased coordination and better posture, more energy and stamina

Cognitive:

- Academic ability and interests vary greatly
- Thinking and pondering with periods of introspection

Emotional:

- Same sex best friend, leading to strong friendship bonds
- Highly "romantic" period for boys and girls
- May be moody, unpredictable and inconsistent
- This is a period of highs and lows and loneliness characterized by turmoil with parents in their bid for independence as peer group is becoming more important as a socializing agent.

Young Adulthood has the developmental task of achieving INTIMACY vs ISOLATION and the psychosocial strength characterized by successful achievement of this developmental task is LOVE and ATTACHMENT.

Older Adulthood has the developmental task of achieving GENERATIVITY vs STAGNATION and the psychosocial strength characterized by successful achievement of this developmental task is CARING and HELPING.

Old Age has the developmental task of achieving INTEGRITY vs DESPAIR and the psychosocial strength characterized by successful achievement of this developmental task is WISDOM and WHOLENESS.

APPENDIX II

CAREER CHOICE

TABLE OF CONTENTS

6. Basic Career Assessment II (<u>Personal Dimension)</u>

    1. TJ TA (Taylor-Johnson Temperament Analysis) (PAR)
    2. MBTI (Myers-Briggs Type Indicator) (CPP)
    3. RIAS (Reynolds Intellectual Assessment Scales) (PAR)
    4. CPI-434 (California Psychological Inventory) (CPP)

7. Test Instruments and Surveys (<u>Family Dynamics)</u>

    1. GZTS (Guilford-Zimmerman Temperament Survey) (PSYCHCORP)
    2. CAIR (Clinical Assessment of Interpersonal Relationships) (PAR)
    3. OPI (Omni Personality Inventory) (PAR)
    4. CPCI (Chronic Pain Coping Inventory) (PAR)

8. Assessment of Learning Style and Performance Abilities

    1. MBTI (Myers-Briggs Type Indicator) (CPP)
    2. CAPS (Career Ability Placement Survey) (Edits)
    3. WRAT4-Expanded (Wide Range Achievement Test) (PAR)
    4. RIAS (Reynolds Intellectual Assessment Scales) (PAR)

9. The Quest for Suitable Employment

WHY CAREER ASSESSMENT

The purpose of career testing is to assist the client in the quest for interesting and enjoyable work and maximizing one's effectiveness in the job market. It is particularly important in today's labor market for an individual to have a firm grasp of his/her personal abilities and personality features as they relate to the "World of Work." Because the current work environment in American economic society is undergoing so much change, instability, and "downsizing" it is more important than ever to be girded for strong job competition. Many have been finding out that jobs are no longer secure with a good pair of hands and company loyalty. There is much that one must know about oneself, in addition to acquired skills, in order to be prepared for today's market economy.

The knowledge, training and skills for employment are intended to be provided through formal education or trade schools however, in addition, one must have self-awareness and self-confirmation of one's personal work-place strengths and weaknesses which can be obtained from career assessment and consultation. Such an endeavor is a way of planning realistically for a successful career. Assessment includes a measurement of one's relative strengths, assets and weakness as they relate to the work environment in the following dimensions: general state of well-being and coping behavior, interest orientation to the "world of work," learning and performance style, interpersonal adaptation, potential stress points and incentive values within the work environment, temperament, basic work-place and/or academic skills, work-place values, and intellectual abilities.

These testing procedures have been well established and are in current professional use. They are designed to assist the client in the process of making a suitable career choice and also in assisting employers and managers in fitting employees to more productive and mutually compatible job placements.

As in any such testing process, the results can be spuriously influenced by internal factors such as current state of health and/or emotional status, the effects of mind altering substances or disturbances. Results can also be influences by external factors such as the immediate test environment and interpersonal dynamics or quality of rapport between the tester and the one being tested. If such deleterious influences are currently affecting the client's test behavior, then a course of professional counseling would be recommended prior to a career evaluation.

As pointed out by John L. Holland, Ph.D. in his book, "Making Vocational Choices," "Maladaptive career development probably occurs in one or more of seven major ways."

1. A person has had insufficient experience to acquire well-defined interests, competencies, and self-perceptions.

2. A person has had insufficient experience to learn about the major kinds of occupational environments.

3. A person has had ambiguous, conflicting, or depreciative experience about his or her interests, competencies, and personal characteristics.

4. A person has acquired ambiguous, conflicting, or depreciative information about the major work environments.

5. These and other deficiencies make it difficult to translate personal characteristics into occupational opportunities. All four probably contribute to a diffuse sense of identity so that choosing an occupation or changing jobs within a career is more uncertain. So that choosing or changing jobs within a career is more uncertain. In addition, many other variables make the translation task difficult or very time consuming. Some people simply have a slow rate of personal development and are slow in developing a well-defined profile of interests and competencies, or they may have a complex outlook so that decisions are made slowly. Still others may be so alienated that they are uninvolved with work or deny the need to choose. And for a few people, neuroticism and pathology make job choosing, changing, and holding precarious; for these tasks like the other major problems of life, require effective interpersonal skills and some emotional stability.

6. Some persons lack the personal, educational, or financial resources to carry out their plans.

7. Some persons with consistent and differentiated profiles, and with a clear sense of identity, are unable to find congruent work due to economic or social barriers. The availability or work of different types is determined by the socio-traditional nature of the economy, cultural values, stages in the economic cycle, and traditional definitions of sexual or ethnic roles. And hard times reduce both job opportunities and career assistance resources of all kinds.

Holland goes on to indicate that such deficiencies, "probably require career counseling, a career course or workshop, and perhaps psychotherapy to resolve some gross misperceptions of self and the world." Therefore, between the extremes of one who has a well differentiated and consistent interest profile with congruent aspirations and one who does not, it is important to determine the specific kinds of information, experience, or clarification that a person needs. The client's history interview prior to testing will usually lend support to the interpretations and overall veracity of the assessment. This procedure analyzes the client's behavioral style and ways of doing things. Can the results be expected to be completely correct? Perhaps yes, perhaps maybe. Test results and information gleaned from interviews suggest behavioral tendencies and patterns in adult life but cannot be thought to be cast in stone. One must feel free to delete any statement or result from the assessment that may not apply, but only after checking with other sources such as friends, relatives or colleagues.

Assessment data are presented as to the relative significance of the test scores and how they conform to the average or extend beyond the average in either direction of high or low. The following is a description of the tests used in this assessment paradigm.

ASSESSMENT RESOURCES:

Pearson Clinical Assessment and PsychCorp
    P.O. Box 1416, Minneapolis, MN 55440
    Phone: 1-800-627-7271
    P.O. Box 599700, San Antonio, TX 78259
    Phone: 1-800-211-8378

Professional Assessment Resources:
    16204 N. Florida Ave. Lutz, FL 33549
    Phone: 1-800-331-8378
    Consulting Psychologists Press:
    1055 Joaquin Road, 2nd Floor Mountain View,
    CA 94043
    Phone: 1-800-624-1765

Mind Gardens, Inc.:
    855 Oak Grove Ave. Suite 215 Menlo Park, CA
    94025
    Phone: 1-650-322-6300

Edits:
    P.O Box 7234
    San Diego, CA 92167
    Phone: 1-800-416-1666

CAREER EVALUATION SURVEY

Name: Age: Date:

Please consider in what general area of occupational endeavor you would find yourself most comfortable.

1. Are you sure of your occupational goals? Do you know what kind of work you would find interesting and satisfying?	Yes	No
2. Do you understand the kind of skills and training required to succeed in your occupational objectives?	Yes	No
3. Are you uncertain about your occupation goals and objective but have some notions and feel a need for some confirmation? Would you like some assistance in this?	Yes	No
4. Are you completely uncertain about what directive to take in terms of occupational goals and objectives and want some help?	Yes	No

1. Realistic/Motoric: Those in this occupational mode regard themselves as practical-minded and people with interests that tend to lie in mechanical skills, realism, and practically but may show deficits in inter-personal skills and sensitivity to their own or other's feelings. They enjoy constructing things and operating types of machinery or vehicles. They basically enjoy working with their hands. However, this does not exclude other interests as well.

2. Investigative/Scientific: These individuals are concerned with science, mathematics, and history. They prefer to "think through" problems rather than "act them out," "They are

motivated by curiosity and need to investigate. They tend to be bright, scholarly, and persistent and can have high academic aspirations and value aesthetics. They can be less interested in social, political or business activities but not necessarily so. They may pursue occupations such as medical science, physics, or research and may become overly preoccupied with their own ideas and opinions.

3. Artistic/Aesthetic: Imagination and creativity characterize these individuals. They tend to value self-expression, originality and unconventionality. They may be over-anxious, complex, and can be emotionally insecure. They are usually driven by a search for creative expression in one form of another whether it be music, writing, or drama, for example. They can also be unstable and subject to emotional difficulties if they fail to find suitable ways to express themselves.

4. Social/Supportive: These individuals prefer roles such as teaching or some form of therapeutic endeavor. They see themselves as responsible, acceptance of feelings, facile and insightful in interpersonal relationships. They tend to solve problems by means of feelings rather than intellectualizing. They are also highly introjective of moral standards and religious values. They see themselves as understanding and wanting to help others but may tend toward over-dependency.

5. Conventional/Conforming: This type tends toward conventional standards, traditions, status and ethnocentrism. They prefer

structured roles with replicable, verbal and numerical activities. They prefer adherence to rules and well-ordered life styles. They wish to avoid conflict and anxiety that is aroused by ambiguous situations and problems of interpersonal relationships. There is generally a whole-hearted uncritical acceptance of cultural values and attitudes and a living in the eyes of others with its emphasis on self-control. They can become overly obsessive and compulsive with order, and regulations. They are drawn toward occupations such as book-keeping, accounting, banking, military and government service.

6. Enterprising/Persuasive: These individuals tend to see themselves as dominant, sociable, cheerful and adventurous. They also enjoy leadership roles and persuasive activities such as law, starting and managing a business, or political endeavors. They are more tolerant and perhaps stimulated by verbal tasks and ambiguities rather than structured and predictable activities. They strive for power and influence. They can also go to extremes of euphoric elation to depression.

Question:

Of all the six (6) personality types that were described above which would you say is the one that most described you and your interests? What would be the second and third choice?

First Preference:
Second Preference:
Third Preference:

What things do you enjoy doing or have done that substantiates your preferences?

SCHOOL HISTORY SURVEY

Name:_____ Age:_____ Sex:_____
Date:_____

Academic History: (high school)

Academic motivation: High Average Low
Socialization skills: High Average Low

Highest grade completed:_____

Extra-curriculum activities:
Special interests, talents, skills:
Significant work history:
Satisfying experiences:

Dissatisfying experiences:
Significant social history:
Satisfying experiences:
Dissatisfying experiences:

Social skills or deficits:
Frustrated aspirations and why:
Family and parent-child relationships:
Health, Medical and Developmental History:
Social/Emotional development:
Early school experiences:

WELLNESS EVALUATION OF LIFESTYLE- Holistic Model

(a) Measures wellness in areas of:

> Spirituality
> Self-Direction
> Work and Leisure
> Friendship
> Love

(b) Assessment of Anxiety (Beck Anxiety Inventory) Measures anxiety as:

> Having panic disorder with agoraphobia,
> Panic disorder without agoraphobia,
> Social phobia,
> Obsessive-compulsive disorder
> Generalized anxiety.

(c) Assessment of Depression (Beck Depression Inventory)

> Measures depression as:
> Cognitive/affective
> Somatic/vegetative

COUNSELING
EVALUATION SURVEY

Health, Medical and Developmental History
Intellectual Functioning
Socioeconomic Conditions
Self-Perception and Dispositions
Personal Values and Purposes
Adaptive Functioning and response to Present
Involvement
Social Developmental Factors

THE BASIC CAREER ASSESSMENT 1

(The Work-Place Dimension)

(A) The Holland Vocational Preference Inventory (VPI) measures interest values in six major categories, i.e. realistic/motoric, intellectual/scientific, social/supportive, artistic/aesthetic, enterprising/persuasive, and conventional/conforming. From these results a VPI code is derived and compatible occupational clusters are suggested.

(a) The Career Assessment Inventory-Enhanced (CAI) compares an individual's occupational interests to those of individuals in 111 specific careers that reflect a broad range of technical and professional positions in today's workforce. It is composed of widely accepted models of Realistic, Investigative, Artistic, Social, Enterprising, and Conventional. The general occupational themes are further divided into 25 inclusive occupational scales. These occupational scales match an individual's likes and dislikes to those of people who have been satisfactorily employed in occupations for a number of years. The occupational scales include skilled trades, service professions and professional occupations. Non occupational scales include: Educational Orientation, Fine Arts-Mechanical, Occupational Extroversion/Introversion, and Variability of Interests.

(B) The Career Orientation Placement and Evaluation Schedule (COPES) measures work-place values in the following dimensions:

- INVESTIGATIVE and CHALLENGED rather than ACCEPTING of activities with concrete results and no need to solve complex problems.
- Promoting PRACTICAL and EFFICIENT ways of doing things rather than CAREFREE and EXPECTING OTHERS to take care of equipment and keep things in good working order.
- Prefers INDEPENDENCE from rules, regulations and social conventions and the freedom to work on their own rather than the CONFORMITY of working under careful supervision where clear directions and regulations can be followed.
- Prefers a LEADERSHIP role in making decisions, directing others, and speaking for the group rather than a SUPPORTIVE role in which they can be good followers and do not need to direct others or tell others what to do.
- Prefers ORDERLINESS and KEEPING THINGS NEAT AND TIDY AND IN THEIR PROPER PLACE rather than being NON-COMPULSIVE in which they can take things as they come and do not need to keep things orderly and neat.
- A desire for RECOGNITION and the wish to become WELL KNOWN and FAMOUS rather than keeping their activities to themselves and VALUING THEIR PRIVACY.

- Prefers the APPRECIATION AND ENJOYMENT OF AESTHETIC AND MUSICAL VALUES and the cultivation of artistic skills and a sense of intuition rather than a preference for REALISTIC ACTIVITIES in which the senses are used and things and objects can be manipulated such as machinery.
- A preference for the SOCIAL in which helping others and working in a friendly environment is valued rather than activities in which SELF-INTEREST is paramount and time is spent on their own projects and tending to their own affairs.

(C) The fundamental Interpersonal Relations Orientation-Behavior (FIRO-B) Assesses how personal needs affect a client's behavior toward other people. It examines the way the client interacts with others, and the way the client wishes others to interact with him/her in the following dimensions:

INCLUSION—-determines the extent of contact and prominence an individual seeks to express and wishes from others.

CONTROL—-determines the extent of power or dominance that a person seeks to express and wishes from others.

AFFECTION—-determines the extent of affection that a person seeks to express and wishes from others.

(D) The Work Environment Scale— (Real, Ideal and Expected)

Measure an employee's perception of the work environment and helps to evaluate productivity; assess employee satisfaction; and clarify employee work expectations to ensure a healthy and compatible work environment.

The specific dimensions assessed on the WES are:

Relationships on the job;
Personal growth;
Goal orientation;
System maintenance; and System change.

THE BASIC CAREER ASSESSMENT II

(The Personal Dimension)

(A) Taylor-Johnson Temperament Analysis (T-JTA)

Measures traits on a continuum from:

Nervous to Composed
Depressive to Light Hearted
Active Social to Quiet
Expressive-Responsive to Inhibited
Sympathetic to Indifferent
Subjective to Objective
Dominant to Submissive
Hostile to Tolerant
Self-Disciplined to Impulsive

(B) The Myers-Briggs Type Indicator (MBTI):

Measures psychological performance style such as introvert vs. extrovert, feeling vs thinking, sense responsive vs. intuitive, and a preference for judging events vs perceiving them without judgment. These indices can show how an individual would contribute to an organization, demonstrate leadership qualities, show preferences for work environments, indicates potential pitfalls, and present suggestions for development.

(C) THE REYNOLDS INTELLECTUAL ASSESSMENT SCALES (RIAS):

Provides an objective, reliable assessment of intelligence and its major components which include:

A two Subtest Verbal Intelligence Index (verbal analytical reasoning and vocabulary knowledge in combination with reasoning skills that are predicated on language development and fund of information)

A two-subtest Nonverbal Intelligence Index (general reasoning skills emphasizing nonverbal ability and nonverbal reasoning skills through the presentation of pictures in which some important component of the picture object is missing)

Also, a Composite Intelligence Index is created by combining the VIX and NIX subtests. In addition, the RIAS provides assessments of Organic Syndrome such as Alzheimer's disease or Parkinson's disease, Mental Retardation, Learning Disability, ADHD and Psychiatric disorders such as anxiety, depression, schizophrenia, bipolar disorder and polysubstance abuse.

(D) THE CALIFORNIA PSYCHOLOGICAL INVENTORY (434)

Measures normal social attributes in the following dimensions:

- Interpersonal Style and Manner of Dealing With Others:

Measures poise, ascendency and self-assurance specifically in areas of Dominance, Capacity for Status, Sociability, Social Presence, Self-Acceptance, Independence and Empathy.

- Internalization and Endorsement of Normative Conventions:
  Measures socialization, maturity and responsibility specifically in the areas of:
  Responsibility, Socialization, Self-Control, Good Impression, Communality, Tolerance and Well Being.
- Cognitive Intellectual Functioning:
  Measures achievement via Conformity, Achievement via Independence, and Intellectual Efficiency.
- Thinking and Behavior
  Measures intellectual and interest modes specifically in the areas of Psychological-Mindedness, Flexibility and Masculinity/ Femininity interests.

When the assessments are completed, a summary session of consultation and interpretative material is provided to assist the client in bringing together the relevant information into a coherent and purposeful understanding of his/her personality features and how they relate to the work environment.

TEST INSTRUMENTS AND SURVEYS (Family Dynamics)

(A) Guilford-Zimmerman Temperament Survey
Measures such traits as:

> General Activity (energy level)
> Restraint (emotional maturity)
> Ascendance (control/manipulation)
> Sociability (gregariousness)
> Emotional Stability (behavior/feeling)
> Objectivity (emotional detachment)
> Friendliness (Amiability)
> Thoughtfulness (observe/analyze/reflect)
> Personal Relations (tolerance/understanding)
> Masculinity (gender specific interest values)

(B) Clinical Assessment of Interpersonal Relationships (Bruce A. Bracken, Ph.D.)

Measures perceptions that youths between the ages of 9-19 years (Grade 5-12) have regarding the quality of their relationships with the most important individuals in their lives—-mother, father, male and female peers, and teachers, in three primary contexts (Social, Family, and Academic)

> The CAIR is a psychometrically sound instrument based on Dr. Bracken's multidimensional, context-dependent model of adjustment. It helps with the early identification and remediation of a youth's relationship difficulties and assists with the identification of

Emotional Disturbance by assessing the quality of the youth's primary relationships.

The CAIR is composed of 35 items, all of which appear on each of five scales (Mother scale, Father scale, Male Peers scale, Female Peers scale, and Teachers scale). All or a select number of scales may be administered. Additionally, the CAIR items reflect the 15 specific aspects of relationship that are commonly reported in the literature, thereby helping the clinician to identify the specific relationship qualities that may be deficient and that may require intervention.

OMNI Personality Inventory:

(C) The OMNI measures both normal and abnormal personality traits. The OMNI assesses 25 normal traits (Normal scales) and 10 abnormal traits (Personality Disorder scales). The Personality Disorder scales are based on the DSM-IV Axis II personality disorder criteria. A Variable Response Inconsistency (VRIN) scale identifies item response inconsistencies and a Current Distress (CD) scale assesses the respondent's mental state during the 7 days prior to the test date.

(D) SURVEY OF PAIN ATTITUDE (SOPA)
CHRONIC PAIN COPING INVENTORY (CPCI)

Measures of a patient's pain copying strategies, attitudes and beliefs about pain.

SOPA consists of seven scales and two domains:

Scales: (Maladaptive Beliefs Domain)

Disability—patients belief he/she is disabled

Harm—belief that pain is signal of physical damage

Medication—belief that meds are appropriate treatment

Solicitude—belief that others should be helpful

Scales: (Adaptive Belief Domain)

Control—see self as having control over pain

Emotion—belief that emotion has impact on pain

CPCI consists of nine scales that are divided into two Domains

Scales: (Illness-Focused Coping Domain)

Guarding—extent of patient's motion restriction

Resting—extent of patient's pain-contingent

Asking for Assistance—frequency of asking for help

Scales: (Wellness-Focused Coping Domain)

Exercise/Stretch—how many days patient stretches

Relaxation—frequency patient uses strategies for rest

Task Persistence—extent patient continues normal activity

Coping Self-Statements—use of adaptive cognitions

Pacing—extent patients paces activities

Seeking Social Support—frequency patient seeks support

ASSESSMENT OF LEARNING STYLE AND PERFORMANCE ABILITY PSYCHOLOGICAL TYPE OR STYLE (Myers-Briggs Type Indicator)

(A) The MBTI is primarily concerned with the valuable differences in people that result from where they like to focus their attention, the way they like to take in information and learn, the way they like to decide, and the kind of lifestyle they adopt.

There is no right or wrong to these preferences. They simply indicate different kinds of people who are interested in different things, are drawn to different fields, and often find some difficulty understanding each other because of the way they focus their attention.

There are eight possible preferences as measure by the MBTI, i.e. Extraversion/ Introversion, Sensing/Intuition, Thinking/ Feeling, and Judgment/Perception. Your type is the combination and interaction of eight preferences that you chose when you completed the MBTI. If we let each preference be represented by its letter then your type can be shown in shorthand by a four-letter code. For example, ISTJ means an introvert (I) who likes to process information with sensing (S), who prefers to use thinking (T) to make decisions, and mainly takes a judging (J) attitude toward the outer world. A person with opposite preferences on all four scales would be an ENFP. This means an extravert (E) who prefers intuition (N) for perceiving, feeling (F) for making decisions, and who takes a perceptive attitude (P) toward the outer world.

CAREER ABILITY AND PLACEMENT SURVEY (CAPS)

(B) The CAPS test measures workplace skills in the following eight dimension: Mechanical Reasoning; Spatial Relations; Verbal Reasoning; Numerical Ability; Language Usage; World Knowledge; Perceptual Speed and Accuracy; and Manual Speed and Dexterity. These abilities are then translated into the following fourteen career cluster: Science, professional; Science, skilled; Technology, skilled; Consumer economics; Outdoor; Business, professional; Business, skilled; Clerical; Communication; Art, professional; Art, skilled; Service, professional; Service, skilled.

BASIC ACADEMIC SKILLS (WIDE RANGE ACHIEVEMENTS TEST 4)

(C) The WRAT4 is a norm-referenced test that measures the basic academic skills, of word reading, sentence comprehension, spelling and math computation. The WRAT4 is useful for:

1. Collecting initial data for psychological, educational and vocational assessments.

2. Permitting time-efficient small group or individual administration in selected math and spelling areas to assist in the identification of individuals who require a more comprehensive academic evaluation.
3. Reevaluating individuals diagnosed with learning and/or cognitive disorders.
4. Contributing to projects needing assessment of basic academic skills for pre-testing and post-testing purposes.
5. Evaluating achievements/ability discrepancies to identify specific learning disabilities.
6. Determining a minimal level of proficiency needed to perform in certain educational and/ or vocational settings.

(D) THE REYNOLDS INTELLECTUAL ASSESSMENT SCALES (RIAS):

Provides an objective, reliable assessment of intelligence and its major Components:

A two subtest Verbal Intelligence Index (verbal analytical reasoning and vocabulary knowledge in combination with reasoning skills that are predicted on language development and fund of information),

A two-subtest Nonverbal Intelligence Index (general reasoning skills emphasizing nonverbal reasoning skills through the presentation of pictures in which some important component of the picture object is missing)

Memory subtest which measure the ability to encode, briefly store, and recall verbally presented material in a meaningful context and the ability to encode, briefly store, and recall visually presented material, whether the stimuli represent concrete objects or abstract concepts.

Also, a Composite Intelligence Index is created by combining the VIX and NIX subtests. In addition, the RAIS provides assessments of Organic Syndrome such as Alzheimer's disease or Parkinson's disease, Mental Retardation, Learning Disability/ADHD and Psychiatric disorders such as anxiety, depression, schizophrenia, bipolar disorder and polysubstance abuse.

THE QUEST FOR SUITABLE EMPLOYMENT

1. The Resume
2. Studying the Market
3. Who Do I Want to Work For or Who DO I Want To Service
4. Making the Initial Contact and Preparing for the First interview
5. The Employment Interview
6. Making It All Work For You

I. The Resume

First of all the resume is not for everybody. If you are looking for a part-time summer job in cannery and you find a "Now Hiring" sign on the door you can expect that all one requires of you is willingness to do a simple job and be at work on time. The well thought out resume is about seeking a lifetime commitment to an occupation or profession that will give you a lifetime of satisfaction and money that will enable you to send your kids to college and provide for a comfortable retirement.

The resume is a brief description of who you are prepared to offer as an employee. It must be concise, to the point, and accurate. Therefore, a good resume must not take more than two easily readable pages with the highlights of your work experiences, along with a description of what type of work you are seeking on the first page, and summation of your prior employment history, education and training on the second. All must be focused on the particular employment you are seeking. So that requires that you know something about it before you step in the door of the employer's office.

Most employee interviewers are quite busy and inundated with job seekers of all kinds. They don't want to take the time to figure out from what is on piece of paper what you can do for his/her company. They want it right there in front of them and clear as bell. That means that you must do some researcher of your own to find out just how you may be of service to this particular company. It is important to not only list jobs you have had in the past but specifically how they relate to the job you are seeking. Also, any outstanding recognition you may have received is always appreciated. Be honest. Never pad or exaggerate or distort in order to look good because, like marriage, if two people come together who really do not know each other when they form the relationship, the truth will eventually come out and there can be nothing but trouble.

II. Studying the Market

Today's market place is not only more complex but considerably more unstable than it was in times past. Business and industries flourish and then disappear like the "Rise and Fall of the Roman Empire". But instead of taking centuries, it can happen in a decade or less. When I was growing up in the "40s and 50s", you could set your sights on getting a job with a large company and work there for 30 years and then retire with a predictable pension and retirement benefits. People would plan their whole life around that kind of stability. In recent times we have seen the near demise of the greatest of them all—the great General Motors Corporation. Who would think such a thing could happen in America 50 years ago?

All this goes to show that one entering the job market today must be prepared for many changes throughout a lifetime and stability must come from within oneself by being prepared to provide specific skills regardless of the company or organization one is employed by.

Becoming aware of the market and where you might apply your skills and abilities require some research on your part. The Internet is a wonderful tool and can be used to put you in touch with helpful agencies.

The Government, also, can be accessed for job information such as: The Federal Government; USA Jobs; Government Hobs by Location; Federal Government Jobs and USA.gov. All can be found using GOOGLE search engine on the computer.

III. Who Do I Want to Work For or Who DO I Want To Service

Just as an author must consider the interests of those for whom he is writing, so also must you consider whomever you wish to provide your service for. If you are an artistic type of person with artistic skills, you will probably not want to apply for work in a bank or a bookkeeper. It is important that you not only find a compatible work environment but also a compatible social environment. In looking at personality types, artists are not at all like bookkeepers. What gives each satisfaction on a job is quite different, as you may well imagine. A person who wants to provide a service as a psychotherapist would not be advised to seek employment in an engineering firm; however, when we look at shadings rather than bold colors we might find someone with therapy training interested in working with a Human Resources department of a large manufacturing company doing employee relations work because there can be overlays of compatibility.

Other considerations in seeking compatible employment are the following: Synergistic involvement of management and labor; Coworker cohesion; Supervisor support; Personal autonomy;

Task orientation; Work pressure; Clarity of responsibilities; Managerial control; Encouragement of Innovation; flex time; Exercise facilities; Medical and health protection; Safety features; Maternity leave; Healthy cafeteria offerings; Sick leave; Child care facilities; and Retirement benefits, to name a few. Nothing, of course, is perfect but one must find enough elements of interest in order to devote one's full enthusiasm.

IV. Making the Initial Contact and Preparing for the First interview

It always helps to know someone in the company, so to speak. However, a good way to make an initial contact is by simply making a telephone call to the Human Resources Department of the company you are interested in and asking if it would be possible to have an interview with someone who is doing the kind of work you would like to do. Quite often people like to talk about what they do when someone shows an interest. This way you can have a pleasant chat with someone who can tell you quite a bit about what his/her job entails and more about working for this company in general terms. You ought to go in armed with intelligent questions so as to confirm your legitimate interest and some knowledge of this particular company.

In a day or two it is wise to write a letter of gratitude for the time and information that was given to you. When or if you are invited to have an initial interview with the prospective employer you can refer to the prior interview you had with _____ and how instructive it was. The more you can learn about this company or organization, the better prepared you will be for "snatching the golden ring" when the opportunity arises.

V. The Employment Interview

Well, the moment of truth is here. It's the interview knowledge of your skills, abilities, personality features, intelligence, temperament and a brief, concise statement of your prior job experience. You have also done some of your own investigative work along with a relevant interview with an employee of the company and acquired some important information about the company and the specific job you are seeking. You are now quite clear just how you may fit in and provide a useful service. You have made sure that you are dressed neatly and professionally without being gaudy or ostentatious and you are presenting yourself on time. That's very important. Job interviewers are busy people and don't like to be kept waiting.

When you are called in to the office, look your interviewer in the eye with a smile and offer your hand for a shake. You will be asked to sit down and probably the first thing will be a statement such as, "Tell me about yourself and why you think you would be right for this job" This is a very open question and leaves you much room to organize your thoughts and present an attractive sketch of yourself and what you can do for the company. Usually, in the beginning, it is not a bad idea to thank the interviewer for the opportunity to meet with him/her because you are very interested in working here for the following reasons. You can start by explaining that you had had a prior interview with one of the employees (by name) at your request and learned a great deal, including the overall social environment which you can find every appealing.

You can now relate the specific type of position in which you are interested, what you already know about that position an how you may fulfill those responsibilities and perhaps even add a new dimension or improvement over time.

VI. Making It All Work For You

As in any important relationship it is important to keep a vital, interested, and enthusiastic attitude so being cheerful and optimistic is usually appreciated. Supporting a good social environment is beneficial for you and everyone else because everyone wants to feel appreciate. Controversies and disagreements are bound to come up from time to time but always remember to keep it objective rather than letting anything become personal. A business-like, problem solving stance is one that will be respected. It is also a wise policy to take your business to the next higher level of authority rather than going over someone's head.

Whether or not you prefer to work independently on a project or with a team or under close supervision ought to be clear to you beforehand and an important matter for you to have discussed at the employee interview. It can make a big difference of the effectiveness of your work and the satisfaction of those with whom you are working—and always keep in mind that like a good marriage, what feels right and good for you will probably feel right and good for your employment relations and its purposes. Finally, as Marsha Sinetar says in her book, "Do What You Love, The Money Will Follow," you will not regret a lifetime a satisfaction in making your contribution for the betterment of your society.

APPENDIX III

EMOTIONALLY BONDED RELATIONSHIPS

(From: "Beyond The Love Game"
by Robert Scheid)

WHAT LOVE ISN'T (or the road to
unnecessary suffering):

Fulfillment of all needs.
Waiting for another to make us happy.
Seeking the "perfect" partner.
Criticism
Care-taking.
Giving up individuality.
Dominating.
Suspicion.
Manipulation.
Expectations.
Status seeking.
Hiding your true self.
Possessiveness.
Being a victim.
Security.
Actions incongruent with professed love.

Dishonesty and disloyalty.
An intense high.

WHAT LOVE IS (or the path of aliveness and joy):

An abundant energy; the essence of life.
Appreciation.
Acceptance of imperfection.
Being real.
Genuine living.
Trust.
Partnering.
Openness.
Growth.
Expressing who you are.
Sharing Responsibility.
Risking.
Actions are loving.
Vulnerability.
Joyous contentment.
Devotion.
Work.
Happiness comes from within.
Courage.

WE FEEL LONELY WHEN:

We feel envious of others.
We hold on to anger or bitterness.
We lack confidence or trust in ourselves.

We are fearful of hurt.
We don't share our pain or shame.

We aren't true to ourselves.
We withhold who we truly are.
We become self-absorbed.
We don't relate to those around us.
We don't trust.
We think people are basically bad and the world hostile.
We contract or constrict.

WE FELL CONNECTED WHEN:

We compete only with ourselves.
We feel whatever anger and bitterness arises, then forgive and let go. We focus on our individual uniqueness, appreciating our special place the universe.
We accept pain as part of a rich life, knowing it shall pass.
We risk being ourselves.
We give for the sake of giving.
We notice others, really listening to what they say.
We find points of mutuality to share with those around us.
We develop openness with discernment by listening to our inner voice.
We discover the good in people.
We generate love and acceptance.

YOU KNOW YOU ARE IN LOVE WHEN:

You are certain you have found the "perfect" partner (or one you feel good and right being with).

You magnify the good qualities of your beloved and minimize the flaws.
You feel excited about your life together.
You feel fully alive and spontaneous.
You joyously give your beloved.
You feel connected outside of yourself.
Little things become wondrous

YOU KNOW YOU ARE OUT OF LOVE WHEN:

You realize that you haven't found the "perfect" partner.
You maximize the flaws of your partner and overlook the good qualities.
You return to too much structure and become bored.
You start demanding and taking.
You return to self-absorption now that you have "got" your partner.

CREATING A CONSCIOUS ROMANCE

Slowly discover your partner as a unique and irreplaceable soul.
Appreciate the positive qualities of your partner and yourself and become close by intimately sharing human imperfections.
Feel deeply content (and that can be exciting).
Live as fully as possible each moment.
Be playfully spontaneous, even during structured times.
Life itself is wondrous. Joyously give to your beloved and receive back with gratitude. Never take one another for granted.

PRE-REQUISITE INNER AWARENESS IN ORDER TO CREATE SPIRITUALITY BONDED INTIMACY.

1. Inner Child Work:
   It is necessary to become conscious of the programming from your family, society, gender roles, and life experiences so that you do not knee jerk react to situations. The more aware you become, the less you are to act out in ways harmful to others and yourself.

2. Love yourself.
   It is absolutely true that you cannot love another until you first love (value) yourself. If you don't love yourself, you will never really believe your partner loves you no matter how demonstrative he or she is. Also, in order to be truly (emotionally and spiritually) intimate, you must be vulnerable enough to be open and unguarded. This means risking hurt. You need lots inner security to be able to honestly reveal who you are.

3. Become Intimate With Your Higher Power:
   Surrendering yourself to the God of your understanding has the reward of healing the inner void that many of us have inside. The Universal Love is abundant and accessible to all. When we feel connected to Spirit, we take the demand off of our partner to be all things to us.

4. Flow Your Love to Others Without Expectation:
   Loving people cannot help but attract loving people.

5. Become What You Want to Attract:

In a spiritual partnership, like attracts like. Sharing is the purpose, not compensation for our own perceived lack.

HOW TO FIND A SPIRITUALLY BONDED RELATIONSHIP

The Process of Relinquishment

Spirit level desire requires a spirit level response. It is not a mental process, so throw out checklists. It is not a physical process, so do not go frantically from place to place searching. What is required is surrender of this desire to Spirit.

The paradox is that you must want this love with all your heart and, at the same time, be willing to let go of your desire.

What is meant by relinquishment?

The Universe cannot operate on our behalf unless we are willing to let go. Holding on keeps the matter at an ego level. (Have you ever noticed that you try too hard, it seldom works?)

Releasing must be more than words; it must be with one's heart and soul. We know releasing is complete when we feel the burden of finding the right person lifted from our shoulders. We may notice dissipation of pain and loneliness.

There remains a sense of trust. You no longer are anxious about finding the right person because you have inner knowledge that the universe has accepted your request and that it will be fulfilled in divine order.

Go on with your life doing the things you love, being good but yourself, giving to others, and staying open.

If you get inner guidance to go to a particular place or take a particular action, by all means follow through.

Remember that relationship will add to the enjoy in your life but will not automatically make you happy. Happiness is an inside job. It seems that others are most attracted to those who manifested wholeness and inner security.

Characteristics of Codependent and Healthy Relationships

Purpose	Codependent	Healthy
Bonding	To get needs met	Mutual Support and love
Seeks in Partner	Compensatory traits	Compatibility
Feeling of Comfort	Validation	Common interests and values
Love	Defined as need	Defined as support and sharing
Attitude toward giving	Gives in order to get	Gives as concern —with balance
Method of Relating	Caretaker & control	Emotionally intimate, sexual
Expression	For self-gratification	For emotional and physical sharing
Self-esteem	Low self-esteem	High self-esteem
Need for approval	By others	By self
Spiritual Expression	Superficial	Some compatibility

APPENDIX IV

A SHORT COURSE ON THE PSYCHOLOGY OF MENTAL HYGIENE

Bruce Atkinson, Ph.D.

Neither circumstances nor other people can make us happy. It is our own perceptions and attitudes regarding self, circumstances, and projected outcomes which determine the feelings. Happiness is a learned thing. The following elements make up happiness, or contentment:

I. A POSITIVE SELF-CONCEPT:

A. A sense of Acceptance-believing that one is receiving:

1. Love (unconditional acceptance)
2. Approval (appreciation)
3. Inclusion (belonging)
4. Relational meaning and purpose (someone to love)

B. A sense of Significance—believing that one has sufficient:

1. Identity

    1. Uniqueness (features which differentiate from others)
    2. Shared ideals/goals/characteristics—group identification
    3. A calling and sense of direction (destiny)

2. Worth

    1. Intrinsic human value (made in God's image, redeemed,
    2. Competence (abilities, skills, achievements)
    3. Purpose and function (life meaning, neediness)

II. A SENSE OF SECURITY:

A. Sufficient Resources—believing that your needs will be met for:

1. Survival; basic needs for food, water, air, rest, shelter
2. Safety and protection for self and loved ones.
3. Healing, growth, and personal development.

B. Hope—positive expectations for the fulfillment of goals.

III. ENJOYMENT:

This is not merely the maximizing of pleasure and the minimizing of pain. While it may include such positive feelings as joy, inner peace, and a sense of satisfaction, it is more related to the development of an attitude of appreciation (gratefulness) and a sharing of those things and activities that one appreciates.

IV. ACCURATE ATTRIBUTION:

How we perceive the causes of our successes and failures determine much about how we function and how we feel. If our attributions (perceptions/ interpretations) are realistic, then we will be able to prepare and adapt and function successfully. Reality will never completely let us down. If we blame others for our unhappiness, we are deceiving ourselves. If we expect them to provide what we think will make us happy, we will become angry at them and we will try to manipulate them to give us our due. This is always too much pressure for the other to handle, to put us first, and will drive them away. They really do not have the power to make us happy; that remains the business between self and God. If we believe too much in self-power (as in humanism and religious legalism), we become vulnerable to egoistic pride (if we happen to achieve our goals) or self-condemnation (if we fail to achieve our goals). Therefore, a faith-based attribution (which credits God accurately) will necessarily place our own efforts in the proper perspective, leading to both self-acceptance, and also true humility.

APPENDIX V

National Education Association Journal, 1938

RATING TEACHERS' PERSONAL EFFECTIVENESS

IN GETTING STUDENT RESPONSE

1. TEACHER—Genuinely interested in students as persons; enthusiastic; vital.
   STUDENTS—Wholehearted in response (physical and mental alertness)
2. TEACHER—Dynamic and purposeful; interested in student effort.
   STUDENTS—Generally in rapport with teacher.
3. TEACHER—Varying from direct interest in students to obliviousness of students.
   STUDENTS—Varying from eager responsiveness to wandering and inattentiveness/
4. TEACHER—More concerned with routine than for students, unanimated.
   STUDENTS—Listless, conforming dully, showing little concern for teacher.
5. TEACHER—Apathetic, dull, disregarding student purposes.
   STUDENTS—Ignoring teacher finding interest in each other; noisy and careless.

IN CREATING A FRIENDLY CLASSOOM ATMOSPHERE

1. TEACHER—Conversational, friendly and sense of humor; seeing a student point of view.
   STUDENTS—Meeting teacher naturally and with a freely person to person relationship.
2. TEACHER—Friendly, with an understanding adult point of view.
   STUDENTS—Respectful; obedient; willingly conforming.
3. TEACHER—Serious, reserved and exacting;; stirring up competitive effort.
   STUDENTS—Concentrated on own purposes; "touchy", cross acting.
4. TEACHER—Aloof, "talking down" to students; impatient with interruptions digressions.
   STUDENTS—Intolerant and strained; rude to teacher and others.
5. TEACHER—Critical, fault finding, harsh and unfriendly
   STUDENTS—Uncertain; covering up embarrassment.

ESTABLISHING A FEELING OF SECURITY

1. TEACHER—Encouraging, constructive and stimulating; confidence inspiring.
   STUDENTS—Willing to try; undisturbed by mistakes; participating with ease.

2. TEACHER—Constructive in guiding student effort.
   STUDENTS—Most students willingly participating.
3. TEACHER—Overlooking opportunities for "bringing out" weaker students.
   STUDENTS—Capable, self-confident students monopolizing opportunities and weaker students not responding.
4. TEACHER—Permitting students to laugh at mistakes or others or be overly critical.
   STUDENTS—Uncertain, covering up embarrassment in various ways.
5. TEACHER—Intolerant of mistakes; demanding; critical.
   STUDENTS—Afraid to try; self-conscious; restrained or rebellious.

IN EXERTING A STABILIZING INFLUENCE

1. TEACHER—Equal to varying demands; courteous and poised in voice and manner.
   STUDENTS—Controlling voices; courteous; considerate of others.
2. TEACHER—Poised but with evident effort.
   STUDENTS—Generally attentive to task; cooperative with each other and to teacher.
3. TEACHER—Occasionally rushed, impatient and discourteous to students.
   STUDENTS—At times undirected; abandoning tasks; whole class noisy and disorganized.
4. TEACHER—Indecisive, uncertain, distracted; tom between several demands.

STUDENTS—Impatient with each other; quarrelsome, irritable.

5. TEACHER—Flustered, hurried, rushing; strained, impatient, lacking central Purposes.
    STUDENTS—Using shrill voices, noisy, blustering, selfish, rude; demanding attention.

INSPIRING ORIGINALITY AND INITIATIVE

1. TEACHER—Original in manner; ingenious, resourceful.
    STUDENTS—Responsive to extent of offering ideas and with enthusiasm.
2. TEACHER—Motivating work through use of interesting devices and aids.
    STUDENTS—Showing interest and willingness to participate.
3. TEACHER—Using an habitual procedure; possessing typical classroom mannerism.
    STUDENTS—Following in a routine way; showing little initiative.
4. TEACHER—No variation in language; dull; prosaic.
    STUDENTS—Bored acting and half-hearted; without purpose or direction.
5. TEACHER—Wholly lacking in ability to intrigue the students.
    STUDENTS—Wholly apathetic and dull; a prevalent "I don't care attitude."

IN DEVELOPING STUDENT SELF-RELIANCE

1. TEACHER—Entering into student activities without domination; exchanging ideas, encouraging student decision making.
   STUDENTS—Initiating; suggesting ways and means; solving problems.
2. TEACHER—Putting students "on their own;" guiding and suggesting.
   STUDENTS—Accepting responsibility in terms of teacher's suggestions.
3. TEACHER—Expecting students to "try for themselves" but over-solicitous, hovering and protective; unwilling to trust student judgment.
   STUDENTS—Over-anxious about results; constantly referring to teacher.
4. TEACHER—In didactic manner, telling students exactly each step to take.
   STUDENTS—Relying on teacher showing exactly each step to take; little ability to think for themselves.
5. TEACHER—Apart, removed, giving "long distance" directions; demanding conformity.
   STUDENTS—Assuming no responsibility; showing practically no concern for own actions; uncontrolled.

APPENDIX VI

AN EXTRACT FROM THE BOOK, "FAILING FORWARD"

by John C. Maxwell

The main difference between people who achieve and those who are average or un-achieving:

Failing Backward	Failing Forward
(a) Blaming others	Taking responsibility
(b) Repeating the same mistakes	Learning from each other mistake
(c) Expecting never to fail again	Knowing failure is part of the process
(d) Expecting to continually fail	Maintaining a positive attitude
(e) Accepting tradition blindly	Challenging outdated assumptions
(f) Being limited by past mistakes	Taking new risks
(g) Thinking I am a failure	Believing something didn't work
(h) Quitting	Persevering

1. Learn A New Definition of Failure

   Mistakes don't define failure—they are merely the price of achievement on the success journey.
   People thinking failure is avoidable—it is not.
   Rule#1 You will learn lessons.
   Rule#2 There are no mistakes, only lessons.
   Rule#3 A lesson is repeated until it is learned.
   Rule#4 If you don't learn the easy lessons, they get harder. (Pain is the way the universe gets your attention)
   Rule#5 You'll know you've learned a lesson when your actions change.

2. People Think Failure Is An Event—it is not.

   Success is a process. It has to do with knowing your purpose in life, growing to reach your potential, sowing seeds that benefit others and managing well your relationships.

3. People Think Failure Is An Objective—it is not.

   You are the only one who can really label what you do failure. Three steps forward and two steps back is still progress and mistakes are only points of learning.

4. People Think Failure is the Enemy—it is not.

   When we permit ourselves to fail we also permit ourselves to excel.

5. People Think Failure is Irreversible—it is not.

   There's an old saying in Texas, "It doesn't matter how much milk you spill as long as you don't lose your cow." Tom Peters said, "If silly things were not done, intelligent things would never happen."

6. People Think Failure is a Stigma—it is not.

   The average for entrepreneurs is 3.8 failures before they finally make it in business.

7. People Think Failure is Final—it is not.

   It's all in how you look at it. It's not an event successful or unsuccessful but how you think about it. Failure is simply a price we pay to achieve success. Washington Irving once said, "Great minds have purposes; others have wishes. Little minds are subdued by misfortunes; but great minds rise above them."

BIBLIOGRAPHY

Baker, Russ (2009), Family of Secrets; The Bush Dynasty, The Powerful Forces That Put It in The White House, and What Their Influence Means For America, New York, BloomsburyPress

Baron, Renee (1998), What Type am I? The Myers-Brigg Type Indication Made Easy, New York, Penguin Books

Beattie, Melody (1986), Codependent No More; How To Stop Controlling Others and Start Caring For Yourself, Center City, Minnesota, Hazelden

Bennett, William J. (1993), The Book of Virtues; New York, Simon & Shuster Paperbacks

Beven, Gerald; translator (2003), Alexis De Tocqueville, Democracy in America; New York, Penguin Classics

Bradley, Bill (2007), The New American Story; New York, Random House Bradshaw, John, (1987), On The Family; Deerfield Beach, Florida Health Communications, Inc.

Bradshaw, John (2009), Reclaiming Virtue; New York, Bantam Dell Press

Brehony, Kathleen A. (1996), Awakening at Midlife; New York, Riverhead Books

Buchanan, Patrick J. (2006), State of Emergency; The Third World Invasion and Conquest of America, New York, Thomas Dunne Books

Burns, David D. M.D. (1980), Feeling Good. The New Mood Therapy: New York, HarperCollins Publishers

Carnegie, Dale (1936), How to Win Friends and Influence People; New York, Simon & Shuster, Inc.

Cloud, Henry and Townsend, John (1999), Boundaries in Marriage; Grand Rapids, Michigan, Zondervan Publishing House

Coontz, Stephanie (1992), The Way We Never Were; American Families and the Nostalgia Trap, New York, Basic Books

Diagnostic Critera: DSM IV. (2000), Washington DC, American Psychiatric Association

Dictionary of Occupational Titles. (2003). U.S. Department of Labor, Franklin, New Jersey, Career Press

Donald, David Herbert (1995), Lincoln; New York, NY, Simon & Schuster

Dorgan, Senator Byron L. (2006), Take This Job and Ship It; How Corporate Greed And Brain Dead Politics Are Selling Out America, New York, Thomas Dunn Books

Draut, Tamara (2005), Strapped: Why America's 20- and 30-Somethings Can't Get Ahead, New York, Doubleday

Drucker Peter F. and Joseph A. Maciariello (2005), The Effective Executive: New York, HarperCollins Publishing

Elgin, Duane, (1993), Voluntary Simplicity; Toward A Way Of Life That Is Outwardly Simple, Inwardly Rich, New York, William Morrow and Company

Erikson, Erik, and Robert Coles, M.D. (2001), The Erik Erikson Reader; New York, W.W. Norton & Company

Erikson, Erik, (1969), Gandhi's Truth; New York, W.W. Norton & Company Inc.

Erikson, Erik, (1950), Childhood and Society; New York, W.W. Norton & Company, Inc.

Fisk, Robert (2007), The Great War for Civilization; The Conquest of the Middle East, New York, Vantage Press

Fiske, Edward (1992), Smart Schools. Smart Kids; New York, Touchstone

Frankl, Viktor E. (2006), Man's Search for Meaning; Boston, Massachusetts, Beacon Press

Freddoso, David (2008), The Case Against Barak Obama: The Unlikely Rise and Unexamined Agenda of the Media's Favorite Candidate, Washington DC, Regnery Publishing Co.

Friedman, Thomas L. (2005), The World Is Flat; A Brief History of the 21st Century, New York, Farrar, Straus and Giroux

Frost, S. E., Jr. (1989), Basic Teachings of the Great Philosophers; New York, Anchor Books

Gingrich, Newt (2008), Real Change: From The World That Fails To The World That Works, Regnery Publishing Co.

Glasser, William (1975), Schools Without Failure; New York, Harper Colophon

Goleman, Daniel (1995), Emotional Intelligence: New York, Random House

Goleman, Daniel (2006), Social Intelligence; New York, Random House

Goodwin, Doris Kearns (1994), NO Ordinary Time; Franklin & Eleanor Roosevelt: The Home Front in World War II; New York, NY; Simon & Schuster Paperbacks

Gotman, John Ph.D. (1995), Why Marriages Succeed or Fail; New York, Simon & Shuster

Gray, John (1999), Children Are From Heaven; Positive Parenting Skills for Raising Cooperative, Confident, and Compassionate Children, New York, HarperCollins, Publisher

Haass, Richard (2023), The Bill of Obligations, Penguin Press

Hales, Dianne & Hales, Robert E., M.D. (1996), Caring For The Mind; The Comprehensive Guide to Mental Health; New York, Bantam Books

Hecker, Lome L. and Wetchler, Joseph L. (2003), An Introduction to Marriage and Family Therapy: New York, The Haworth Clinical Practice Press

Heilbroner, Robert L. (1999), TheWordlyPhilosphers: The Lives, Times and Ideas of the Great Economic Thinkers, New York, NY; Touchstone

Hendrix, Harville, Ph.D., (1988), Getting the Love You Want; New York, Henry Holt & Co.

Hillman, James (1996), The Soul's Code: In Search of Character and Calling, New York, Warner Books, Inc.

Hirsh, Sandra, and Jean Kummerow (1990) Introduction to Type in Organizations: Palo Alto, CA; Consulting Psychologists Press

Holland, John L. Ph.D. (2009), Making Vocational Choices; Lutz, Florida, Psychological Assessment Resources, Inc.

Holt, John (1964), Why Children Fail; New York, Pitman Publishing Co.

Horn, Jan C. (1988), Decorum in the Classroom; Riverside, California, Abba Press

Horney, Karen M.D (1937), The Neurotic Personality of Our Time; New York W.W. Norton & Company, Inc.

Iococca, Lee (2007), Where Have All The Leaders Gone?; New York, Scribner, Inc.

Iserbyt, Charlotte Thomson (1999), The Dumbing Down of America; Ravenna, Ohio, Conscience Press

James, John W., Friedman, Russell (1998), The Grief Recovery Handbook; New York, HarperCollines Publishers

Jencks, Christopher (1972), Inequality: A Reassessment of the Effect of Family and Schooling in America; New York, Basic Books, Inc.

Johnston, David Cay (2008), Free Lunch—How the Wealthiest Americans Enrich Themselves at Government Expense (and stick you with the bill); Penguin Group

Jones, L. Stanson &Butman E. Richard (1991), Modem Psychotherapy; Downers Grove, IL, Intervasity Press

Jongsma, Arthur E. Jr.,& Peterson, L. Mark (1999), The Complete Adult Psychotherapy Treatment Planner; New York, John Wiley & Sons, Inc.

Jongsma, Arthur E. Jr.,& Peterson, L. Mark,&Mcinnis, William P. (2000), The Child Psychotherapy Treatment Planner; New York, John Wiley & Sons, Inc.

Jongsma, Arthur E. Jr.,& Peterson, L. Mark &Mcinnis, William P. (2000), The Adolescent Psychotherapy Treatment Planner; New York, John Wiley & Sons, Inc.

Jung, Carl (1923), Psychological Types; New York, Harcourt Brace

Keirsey, David and Marilyn Bates (1978), Please Understand Me; Del mar, CA: Prometheus Nemesis Books

Kennan, George F. (1972), Memoirs 1950-1963: New
York, Pantheon Books

Kozol, Jonathan (1992), Savage Inequalities: Children in
American Schools; New York, Crown Publishing

Lawrence, Gordon (1979), People Types and Tiger
Stripes: A Practical Guide To Learning Styles,
Gainesville, Florida, Center for Applications of
Psychological Type, Inc.

Lazarus, Arnold A. (1997), Brief but Comprehensive
Psychotherapy; New York, NY Springer Publishing
Company

Lazarus, Arnold A. (1991), Marital Myths; Two Dozen
Mistaken Beliefs That Can Ruin A Marriage
(Or Make A Bad One Worse), San Luis Obispo,
California, Impact Publishers

Lazarus, Arnold A., Ph.D., and Clifford N., Ph.D. (1997),
The 60 Second Shrink: 101 Strategies For
Staying Sane In A Crazy World, San Luis Obispo,
California, Impact Publishers

Lazarus, Arnold A., Ph.D., and Allen Fay, M.D. (1975),
I Can If I Want To: Changing Your Thinking,
Change Your Behavior, Change Your Life; Essex,
Connecticut, FMC BOOKS

Lazarus, Arnold A. Ph.D., (1981), The Practice of
Multimodal Therapy; New York, McGraw-Hill Books

Lazarus, Arnold, Ph.D. and Clifford N. Lazarus, Ph.D.
(1993), Don't Believe It For A Minute; Forty Toxic
Ideas that are Driving You Crazy: Atascadero,
California, Impact Publishers

Lorenz, Konrad (1963), On Agression: New York,
Harcourt Brace Jovanovich, Publishers

Lowman, Rodney L. (1991), The Clinical Practice of Career Assessment: Washington, DC, American Psychological Association

Maltz, Maxwell, M.D. (1960), Pyscho-cybernetics; New York, Pockets Books

Maslow, Abraham (1987), Motivation and Personality; New York, Harper Bros.

Masterson, James F., M.D. (1988), The Search for the Real Self; New York Collier Macmillan, Inc.

Maxwell, John C. (2000), Failing Forward: Turning Mistakes into Stepping Stones for Success: Nashville, Tennessee, Thomas Nelson, Inc.

May, Rollo, (1967), The Art of Counseling; Nashville, Tennessee, Abington Press

McCullough, David (2005), 1776; New York, Simon & Shuster

McGraw, Phil, Ph.D. (2004), Family First: New York, The Free Press

McGreal, Ian P., Edited by (1992), Great Thinkers of the Western World; The major ideas and classic works of more than 100 outstanding Western philosophers, physical and social scientists, psychologists, religious writers, and theologians, New York, NY, HarperCollins Publishers, Inc.

Merrell, Kenneth W., Ervin, Ruth A., Gimpel, Gretchen A. (2006), School Psychology for the 21st Century; New York, The Guilford Press

Meyers, Isabel Briggs, with Mary McCaulley (1985), Manual: A Guide to the Development and Use of the Myers-Briggs Type Indicator; Palo Alto, CA. Consulting Psychologists Press

Michelozzi, Betty Neville (1984), Coming Alive from Nine to Five: Palo Alto, California, Mayfield Publishing Company

Miller, Alice (1997), The Drama of the Gifted Child; New York, HarperCollins Publishers, Inc.

O'Hanlon, Bill & Weiner-Davis, Michele (2003), In search of Solutions: A New Direction in Psychotherapy; New York, W.W. Norton & Company

Obama, Barak (2008), Change You Can Believe In; New York, Three Rivers Press

Obama, Barak (2006), The Audacity of Hope: New York, Crown Publishers

Occupational Outlook Handbook; (2008), U.S. Department of Labor, Skyhorse Publishing, Inc.

Osipow, Samuel H. (1968), Theories of Career Development: New York, Appleton-Century Crofts

Patterson, C.D (1966), Theories of Counseling and Psychotherapy; New York. Harper & Row, Publishers

Peale, Norman Vincent (1948); A Guide To Confident Living; New York, Prentice Hall, Inc.

Peale, Norman Vincent (1952), The Power of Positive Thinking; New York, Simon & Shuster, Inc.

Peck, Scott M., M.D. (1993), Further Along The Road Less Traveled; New York, Simon & Shuster

Piper, Mary, Ph.D. (1994). Reviving Ophelia: Saving the Selves of Adolescent Girls, New York, The Penguin Group

Pollack, William, Ph.D. (1998), Real Bovs. Rescuing Our Sons from the Myths of Boyhood, New York, Henry Holt and Company

Reza, Aslan (2005), No god but God; The Origins, Evolution, and Future of Islam: New York, Random House Trade Paperbacks

Roberts, J.M. (1993), A Short History of the World: New York, Oxford University

Sach, Brad E., Ph.D. (2001), The Good Enough Child; New York, HarperCollins publishers

Seligman, Martin E.P., (1991). Learned Optimism: New York, Simon & Shuster

Selye, Hans, M.D (1974), Stress Without Distress: New York, Harper and Row, Publishers; New York

Sheid, Robert (1980), Beyond The Love Game; Berkely, California, Celestial Arts

Sinetar, Marsha (1987), Do What You Love. The Money Will Follow: New York, Dell Publishing

Smith, Adam (2009), The Wealth of Nations: A Digireads. com Book

Spencer, Robert (2008), Stealth Jihad: How Radical Islam Is Subverting America, Washington DC, Regnery Publishing, Inc.

Sperry, Paul (2005), Infiltration: How Muslim Spies and Subversives Have Penetrated Washington, Nashville, Tennesse, Nelson Current

Stanford, John, Major General, Ret. (1999), Victory in our Schools; We CAN give our Children Excellent Public Education; New York, New York, Bantam Books

Taylor, John F. Ph.D. (2001), From Defiance To Corporation; Real Solutions for Transforming the Angry, Defiant, Discouraged Child, New York, NY Three Rivers Press

Taylor, Maxwell D. General of the Army (1972), Swords and Plowshares A Memoir; New York, NY, Da Capo Press

Tett, Gillian, (2009), Fool's Gold: How the Bold Dream of a Small Tribe at J.P. Morgan was Corrupted by Wall Street Greed and Unleashed a Catastrophe; New York, NY, Free Press

Thompson, Nicholas, (2009), The Hawk and the Dove; Paul Nitze, George Kennan, and the History of the Cold War, New York, NY, Henry Holt and Company

Thoreau, Henry David (1993), Walden and Other Writings; New York, NY, Barnes & Noble, Inc.

Upbike, John (2006), Terrorist: New York, Alfred A. Knopf

Viscott, David M.D. (1976), The Language of Feeling; New York, Arbor House

Webb, Jim (2008), A Time To Fight; New York, Broadway Books

Webster, William G., Sr. (1994), Learner-Centered Principalship: The Principal as Teacher of Teachers; Westport, CT, Praeger Publishers

Weidemer, David Ph.D., Weidemer, Robert A. and Spitzer, Cindy (2011), Aftershock; Protect Yourself and Profit in the Next Financial Meltdown; Hoboken, New Jersey, John Wiley & Sons, Inc.

Weil, Andrew. M.D. (2005), Healthy Aging; New York, Random House

Weinhold, James B.. Ph.D.&Weinhold, Barry, Ph.D. (2008), Flight From Intimacy; Novato, California, The New World Library

Weiten, Wayne, (1986), Psychology Applied to Modem Life; Monterey, California, Brooks/Cole Publishing Co.

Wills, Garry (2010), Bomb Power; The Modem Presidency and the National Security State, New York, NY, The Penguin Press